CIMA

OPERATIONAL LEVEL

PAPER P1

MANAGEMENT ACCOUNTING

FOR EXAMS IN 2018

BPP
LEARNING MEDIA

Fourth edition 2017

ISBN 9781 5097 1579 4
e-ISBN 9781 5097 1591 6

British Library Cataloguing-in-Publication Data
A catalogue record for this book
is available from the British Library

Published by

BPP Learning Media Ltd
BPP House, Aldine Place, 142/144 Uxbridge Road
London W12 8AA

www.bpp.com/learningmedia

Printed in the United Kingdom

Your learning materials, published by BPP Learning
Media Ltd, are printed on paper obtained from
traceable, sustainable sources.

Contents

Question and Answer index

Using your BPP Exam Practice Kit

One of the key criteria for achieving exam success is question practice. There is generally a direct correlation between candidates who study all topics and practise exam questions and those who are successful in their real exams. This Kit gives you ample opportunity for such practice throughout your preparations for your OT exam.

All questions in your exam are compulsory and all the component learning outcomes will be examined so you must **study the whole syllabus**. Selective studying will limit the number of questions you can answer and hence reduce your chances of passing. It is better to go into the exam knowing a reasonable amount about most of the syllabus rather than concentrating on a few topics to the exclusion of the rest.

Practising as many exam-style questions as possible will be the key to passing this exam. You must do questions under **timed conditions**.

Breadth of question coverage

Questions will cover the whole of the syllabus so you must study all the topics in the syllabus.

The weightings in the table below indicate the approximate proportion of study time you should spend on each topic, and is related to the number of questions per syllabus area in the exam.

P1 Management Accounting Syllabus topics	Weighting
A Cost accounting systems	30%
B Budgeting	25%
C Short-term decision making	30%
D Dealing with risk and uncertainty	15%

The Objective Test exam

The Objective Test exam is a computer based assessment (CBA), which is available on demand at assessment centres all year round.

Objective Test exams in each level can be taken in any order, but candidates must pass all the OT exams for a level before they can sit the Integrated Case Study Exam for that level.

Each exam lasts for 90 minutes and the pass mark is 70%.

Results are available shortly after the test has been completed, and the results will include feedback.

The exam will be made up of different types of questions, including:

Question Type	Explanation
Multiple choice	Standard multiple choice items provide four options. 1 option is correct and the other 3 are incorrect. Incorrect options will be plausible, so you should expect to have to use detailed, syllabus-specific knowledge to identify the correct answer rather than relying on common sense.
Multiple response	A multiple response item is the same as a multiple choice question, except more than one response is required. You will normally (but not always) be told how many options you need to select.
Drag and drop	Drag and drop questions require you to drag a "token" onto a pre-defined area. These tokens can be images or text. This type of question is effective at testing the order of events, labelling a diagram or linking events to outcomes.
Gap fill	Gap fill (or 'fill in the blank') questions require you to type a short numerical response. You should carefully follow the instructions in the question in terms of how to type your answer – eg the correct number of decimal places.
Hot spot	These questions require you to identify an area or location on an image by clicking on it. This is commonly used to identify a specific point on a graph or diagram.
Drop-down list	Drop-down lists follow the same principle as multiple choice questions, in that you need to select one option from a pre-defined list. This can be used in conjunction with a gap-fill question: for example, you may be asked to key a numerical answer into a gap-fill box and then select an explanation for the approach you've taken from a drop-down list.

Learning Objectives

The table below has been prepared by CIMA to help you understand the abilities that CIMA is seeking to assess.

Learning objective	Verbs used	Definition	Example question types
1 Knowledge			
What you are expected to know	• List	• Make a list of	MCQ
	• State	• Express, fully or clearly, the details of/facts of	MCQ
	• Define	• Give the exact meaning of	MCQ
2 Comprehension			
What you are expected to understand	• Describe	• Communicate the key features of	Multiple Response
	• Distinguish	• Highlight the differences between	Multiple Response
	• Explain	• Make clear or intelligible/state the meaning or purpose of	Drop down list
	• Identify	• Recognise, establish or select after consideration	Hotspot
	• Illustrate	• Use an example to describe or explain something	Drop down list
3 Application			
How you are expected to apply your knowledge	• Apply	• Put to practical use	Multiple response
	• Calculate/ compute	• Ascertain or reckon mathematically	Number entry
	• Demonstrate	• Prove the certainty or exhibit by practical means	Hotspot
	• Prepare	• Make or get ready for use	Drag and drop
	• Reconcile	• Make or prove consistent/ compatible	Drop down list
	• Solve	• Find an answer to	Number entry
	• Tabulate	• Arrange in a table	Drag and drop
4 Analysis			
How you are expected to analyse the detail of what you have learned	• Analyse	• Examine in detail the structure of	Multiple response
	• Categorise	• Place into a defined class or division	Drag and drop
	• Compare & contrast	• Show the similarities and/or differences between	Hotspot
	• Construct	• Build up or complete	Drag and drop
	• Discuss	• Examine in detail by argument	Multiple response
	• Interpret	• Translate into intelligible or familiar terms	Multiple response
	• Prioritise	• Place in order of priority or sequence for action	Drop down list
	• Produce	• Create or bring into existence	Drag and drop

Learning objective	Verbs used	Definition	Example question types
5 Evaluation			
How you are expected to use your learning to evaluate, make decisions or recommendations	• Advise	• Counsel, inform or notify	Multiple response
	• Evaluate	• Appraise or assess the value of	Multiple response
	• Recommend	• Propose a course of action	Multiple response

In your CBA, questions will be set which test up to the cognitive level of the verb in the component learning outcome in each paper's syllabus, so this means they will test up to level 5 verbs where the learning outcome permits this.

CIMA will limit the number of lower level questions in the exam – so that students will not be able to achieve the pass mark solely based on correctly answering knowledge and comprehension questions. Higher level questions, requiring candidates to demonstrate application, analysis and evaluation skills must be answered correctly for the pass mark to be reached.

Passing the P1 Objective Test exam

Tackling objective test questions (OTQs)

- Read, and **re-read the question** to ensure you fully understand what is being asked.

- When starting to read a question, especially one with a lengthy scenario, **read the requirement first**. You will then find yourself considering the requirement as you read the data in the scenario, helping you to focus on exactly what you have to do.

- **Do not spend too much time on one question** – remember you should spend 1½ minutes, on average, per question.

- If you cannot decide between two answers – look carefully and decide whether for one of the options you are making an unnecessary assumption – **do not be afraid of trusting your gut instinct**.

- **Do not keep changing your mind** – research has shown that the first answer that appeals to you is often the correct one.

- Remember that marks are awarded for correct answers, and marks will not be deducted for incorrect answers. Therefore **answer every single question**, even ones you are unsure of.

- Always submit an answer for a given question even if you do not know the answer – **never leave any answers blank**.

- **Pace yourself** – you will need to work through the exam at the right speed. Too fast and your accuracy may suffer, too slow and you may run out of time. Use this Kit to practise your time keeping and approach to answering each question.

- If you are unsure about anything, remember to **ask the test administrator** before the test begins. Once the clock begins ticking, interruptions will not be allowed.

- Remember to **keep moving on!** You may be presented with a question which you simply cannot answer due to difficulty or if the wording is too vague. If you have only approximately 90 seconds per question, and you find yourself spending five minutes determining the answer for a question then your time management skills are poor and you are wasting valuable time.

- If you finish the exam with time to spare, use the rest of the time to **review your answers** and to make sure that you answered every OTQ.

Demonstrating your understanding of P1

The P1 examiner will expect you to demonstrate the following:

Management accounting knowledge	P1 stresses the importance of costs and the drivers of costs in the production, analysis and use of information for decision making. You will knowledge of the whole syllabus.
Carry out appropriate calculations	You will need to perform calculations that relate to the scenario described in the question.
Make reasonable recommendations	The time focus of P1 is the short term. You will need to make short-term decisions, usually on the basis of calculations.
Understand risk	You will need to show an understanding of the impact of risk when making decisions.

All OTQs in all the exams are worth the same number of marks, both in this Kit and in the real exam. However this is an approximate guide: some OTQs are very short and just require a factual selection, which you either know or you don't, while others are more complex, which will inevitably take more time. Note that the real exam will be balanced such that the 'difficulty' of the exam will be fair for all students – the OTQs in this Kit have also been balanced in a similar way.

Using the solutions and feedback

Avoid looking at the answer until you have finished a question. It can be very tempting to do so, but unless you give the question a proper attempt under exam conditions you will not know how you would have coped with it in the real exam scenario.

When you do look at the answer, compare it with your own and give some thought to why your answer was different, if it was.

If you did not reach the correct answer make sure that you work through the explanation or workings provided, to see where you went wrong. If you think that you do not understand the principle involved, work through and revise the point again, to ensure that you will understand it if it occurs in the exam.

Objective test questions

1a Absorption costing

1a.1 DEF Co publishes three newspapers, The Post, The Gazette and The News. The following information has been obtained from the accounting system for period 6:

	The Post	The Gazette	The News
Number published	60,000	80,000	90,000
Direct labour hours per unit	0.2	0.3	0.1
Machine hours per unit	0.4	0.5	0.3
Set-ups	4	3	3
Distribution outlets	15	18	12

Overheads are related to the following activities:

Activities	Cost of activities
	$
Distribution	22,500
Machine maintenance	24,570
Machine set-up	25,730
	72,800

What is the traditional overhead absorption rate for period 6? (give your answer to 2 dp)

$ ☐

1a.2 **Overheads will always be over-absorbed in which of these circumstances:**

- ☐ Actual output is higher than budgeted output.
- ☐ Actual overheads incurred are higher than the amount absorbed.
- ☐ Actual overheads incurred are lower than the amount absorbed.
- ☐ Budgeted overheads are lower than the overheads absorbed.

1a.3 **Are the following statements about predetermined overhead absorption rates true or false?**

		True	False
(i)	Using a predetermined absorption rate avoids fluctuations in unit costs caused by abnormally high or low overhead expenditure or activity levels.	☐	☐
(ii)	Using a predetermined absorption rate offers the administrative convenience of being able to record full production costs sooner.	☐	☐
(iii)	Using a predetermined absorption rate avoids problems of under/over absorption of overheads because a constant overhead rate is available.	☐	☐

1a.4 A company has over-absorbed fixed production overheads for the period by $6,000. The fixed production overhead absorption rate was $8 per unit and is based on the normal level of activity of 5,000 units. Actual production was 4,500 units.

What were the actual fixed production overheads incurred for the period?

- ☐ $30,000
- ☐ $36,000
- ☐ $40,000
- ☐ $42,000

1a.5 RJD Co operates a standard absorption costing system. The following fixed production overhead data is available for one month:

Budgeted output	200,000 units
Budgeted fixed production overhead	$1,000,000
Actual fixed production overhead	$1,300,000
Total fixed production overhead variance	$100,000 Adverse

The actual level of production was:

☐ 180,000 units
☐ 240,000 units
☐ 270,000 units
☐ 280,000 units

1a.6 A company operates a standard absorption costing system and absorbs fixed production overheads based on machine hours. The budgeted fixed production overheads for the company for the previous year were $660,000 and budgeted output was 220,000 units using 44,000 machine hours. During that year, the total of the fixed production overheads debited to the Fixed Production Overhead Control Account was $590,000, and the actual output of 200,000 units used 38,000 machine hours.

Fixed production overheads for that year were:

☐ $90,000 under absorbed
☐ $60,000 under absorbed
☐ $20,000 under absorbed
☐ $10,000 over absorbed

1a.7 A company produces and sells one type of product. The details for last year were as follows:

Production and sales

	Budget	Actual
Production (units)	25,000	22,000
Sales (units)	23,000	20,000

There was no inventory at the start of the year.

Selling price and costs

	Budget $	Actual $
Selling price per unit	70	70
Variable costs per unit	55	55
Fixed production overhead	130,000	118,000
Fixed selling costs	75,000	75,000

Calculate the actual profit for the year that would be reported using absorption costing.

$ _____

1a.8 **Over-absorbed overheads occur when:**

☐ Absorbed overheads exceed budgeted overheads.
☐ Actual overheads exceed absorbed overheads.
☐ Actual overheads exceed budgeted overheads.
☐ Absorbed overheads exceed actual overheads.

1a.9 A company produced 5,000 units of Product B last month. The opening and closing inventory of Product B was 400 units and 900 units respectively. The selling price and production costs for Product B were as follows:

	$ per unit
Selling price	20.00
Direct costs	6.00
Variable production overhead costs	3.50
Fixed production overhead costs	5.90
Gross profit	4.60

What is the gross profit for Product B last month, using absorption costing?

(Give your answer to the nearest whole $)

$ [   ]

1a.10 A company uses a standard absorption costing system. The fixed overhead absorption rate is based on labour hours.

Extracts from the company's records for the last year were as follows:

	Budget	Actual
Fixed production overhead	$540,000	$570,000
Output	60,000 units	72,000 units
Labour hours	1,080,000	1,110,000

The under or over absorbed fixed production overheads for the year were:

☐ $15,000 under absorbed
☐ $15,000 over absorbed
☐ $30,000 over absorbed
☐ $78,000 over absorbed

1a.11 The following data relate to Product D:

Material cost per unit	$20.00
Labour cost per unit	$69.40
Production overhead cost per machine hour	$12.58
Machine hours per unit	14
General overhead absorption rate	8% of total production cost

What is the total cost per unit of Product D, to the nearest $0.01?

☐ $176.12
☐ $265.52
☐ $286.76
☐ $300.12

1b Activity based costing

1b.1 **Which THREE of the following are used as the basis for absorbing production overheads in a traditional absorption costing system?**

☐ Number of production units
☐ Number of machine hours
☐ Number of labour hours
☐ Number of set ups
☐ Number of quality inspections

1b.2 A company has total overheads of $735,000 of which $488,000 relates to machine use, $85,000 to production set-ups and the balance to handling of orders.

The company has two products X and Y, and expects the following in the next period.

	X	Y
Quantity made	12,000	25,000
Direct labour hours per unit	2	1
Machine hours per unit	3	1
Total number of production set-ups	10	40
Total number of orders	16	20

Using an ABC approach and suitable cost drivers, what is the overhead amount absorbed by each unit of X?

☐ $25.42
☐ $28.50
☐ $31.42
☐ $37.92

1b.3 **Are the following statements relating to activity based costing true or false?**

		True	False
(i)	Activity-based costs can be used to identify relevant costs for short-term decision making.	☐	☐
(ii)	Activity-based costing cannot be used to cost services.	☐	☐
(iii)	Activity-based costing is a form of absorption costing.	☐	☐
(iv)	Activity-based costing is an alternative to traditional volume-based costing methods.	☐	☐

1b.4 A single-product company has the following results for its financial year:

	$'000
Sales	13,000
Direct material costs	(2,600)
Direct labour costs	(1,300)
Fixed overheads	(1,000)
Net profit	8,100

Production for the year was 130,000 units.

The company has performed an activity-based costing exercise and has traced its overheads to the following cost pools:

Cost pool	% of total overhead	Cost driver	Activity level
Order processing	25	Orders processed	50,000
Sales force salaries	40	Sales force hours worked	20,000
Research	35	Department hours worked	10,000

Customer X made 400 orders during the year, required 300 hours of sales force time, 100 hours of research and purchased 1,000 units during the year.

Calculate the profit attributable to customer X under activity-based costing.

☐ $58,500
☐ $60,000
☐ $62,308
☐ $81,000

1b.5 Are the following statements about activity based costing true or false?

	True	False
(i) Short-term variable overhead costs should be traced to products using volume-related cost drivers, such as machine hours or direct labour hours.	☐	☐
(ii) Long-term variable production overhead costs are driven partly by the complexity and diversity of production work, as well as by the volume of output.	☐	☐
(iii) Transactions undertaken by support department personnel are the appropriate cost drivers for long-term variable overhead costs.	☐	☐
(iv) Overheads should be charged to products on the basis of their usage of an activity. A product's usage of an activity is measured by the number ofthe activity's cost driver it generates.	☐	☐

1b.6 The following data relates to production of A Co's three products in period 6.

	Product X	Product Y	Product Z
Production and sales (units)	300	200	150
Machine hours per unit	30	10	10
No. of production runs	7	2	1
No. of quality checks	5	5	5
No. of deliveries of material into store	20	19	1

	$
Machining	35,750
Set-up costs	5,250
Materials handling (receiving)	17,500
Quality check costs	22,500

What is the overhead cost per unit of product Y using activity based costing?

☐ $150.55
☐ $112.91
☐ $525
☐ $2.86

1b.7 Are the following statements true or false?

	True	False
The fixed overhead volume capacity variance represents part of the over/under absorption of overheads	☐	☐
A company works fewer hours than budgeted. This will result in an adverse fixed overhead volume capacity variance	☐	☐

1b.8 A company manufactures two products: M and N. The company is considering changing the method it uses to allocate overheads to products and is looking at implementing an ABC system. Overheads are currently allocated based on labour hours.

	M	N
Production	100,000 units	150,000 units
Materials cost per unit ($)	5	4
Labour cost per unit ($)	25	20
Machine hours per unit	3	2
Number of production checks made	200	600

Fixed overheads of $100,000 are split as follows:

Machining	30%
Set up costs	40%
General admin	10%
Checking	20%

Labour costs $5 per hour. Set up costs are based on the number of production runs and there is a new production run every 500 units. General admin allocation is based on units.

Which of the following is the overhead allocated to one unit of product M under ABC?

☐ $0.36
☐ $0.38
☐ $0.40
☐ $0.45

1b.9 M Co is a furniture manufacturer. One of M Co's products is a chair which is produced in batches of 50.

Chairs go through 11 separate production processes which necessitate a total of 18 materials movements per batch.

There are 30,000 materials movements each year, costing $75,000.

Calculate the activity based cost of materials movements per chair, to the nearest $0.01.

$ [   ]

1b.10 **Which TWO of the following are activity based cost drivers used for?**

☐ Allocate overheads to resources.
☐ Reallocate service cost centre costs to production cost centres.
☐ Allocate overheads to cost objects.
☐ Allocate overheads to production and service cost centres.
☐ Allocate overheads to primary and support activities.

1b.11 JJ plc has recently introduced an activity based costing system. It manufactures three products, details of which are set out below.

	L	D	S
Budgeted annual production (units)	200,000	200,000	100,000
Batch size (units)	200	100	50
Machine set-ups per batch	2	3	5
Purchase orders per batch	3	2	1
Processing time per unit (minutes)	4	5	5

Three cost pools have been identified. Their budgeted costs for the year ending 30 April 20X3 are as follows.

Machine set-up costs	$270,000
Purchasing of materials	$150,000
Processing	$100,000

The budgeted machine set-up cost per unit of product L is nearest to:

☐ $0.54
☐ $0.15
☐ $15
☐ $30

1b.12 Activity based costing (ABC) is claimed to provide more accurate product costs than a traditional absorption costing system.

Which of the following statements does NOT support this claim?

☐ ABC uses cost drivers to allocate overhead costs to products by cost pool
☐ ABC identifies value added and non-value added activities
☐ ABC assigns overheads to each major activity
☐ ABC uses both volume based and non-volume based cost drivers

---

1b.13 A company uses an activity based costing system. Three products are manufactured, details of which are given below:

	Product A	Product B	Product C
Annual production (units)	80,000	100,000	50,000
Batch size (units)	100	50	25
Machine set-ups per batch	3	4	6

Annual machine set-up costs are $150,000.

The machine set-up cost per unit of Product B (to the nearest $0.01) is:

☐ $0.46
☐ $0.65
☐ $6.70
☐ $0.54

1b.14 A company uses an activity based costing system to attribute overhead costs to its three products. The following budget data relates to this year:

Product	X	Y	Z
Production (units)	50,000	25,000	20,000
Batch size	250	100	400

Material handling costs are determined by the number of batches of each product and have been estimated to be $60,000 for the year.

What is the cost driver rate for material handling costs?

Give your answer to the nearest whole $

$ [   ]

1b.15 **Classify the following activity based costs incurred in a multi product manufacturing environment by placing the activities next to the costs below:**

A   Batch level activities
B   Product sustaining activities
C   Facility sustaining activities
D   Unit level activities

Purchase order processing costs   [   ]

Product advertising costs   [   ]

Factory rent and rates   [   ]

Direct labour costs   [   ]

Product redesign costs   [   ]

Material handling costs   [   ]

1b.16 Happy plc makes two products Smile and Tickle. The following information has been given to you:

	Smile	Tickle
Production (units)	400	1,600
Machine hrs/unit	6	8
Production runs	5	2
Inspections (during production)	3	6

Production set up costs	$134,400
Quality control costs	$55,200

Using activity based costing, which of the following is the overhead cost per unit of product Tickle?

☐ $57.20
☐ $47.00
☐ $71.50
☐ $286.00

2 Marginal costing and throughput accounting

2.1   The following details have been extracted from the budget papers of LK plc for June 20X3.

Selling price per unit	$124
Variable production costs per unit	$54
Fixed production costs per unit	$36
Other variable costs per unit	$12
Sales volume	12,500 units
Production volume	13,250 units
Opening inventory of finished items	980 units

If budgeted profit statements were prepared by using absorption costing and then by using marginal costing:

☐   Marginal costing profits would be higher by $27,000
☐   Absorption costing profits would be higher by $27,000
☐   Absorption costing profits would be higher by $35,000
☐   Absorption costing profits would be higher by $62,000

2.2   A company produces and sells one type of product. The details for last year were as follows:

Production and sales

	Budget	Actual
Production (units)	25,000	22,000
Sales (units)	23,000	20,000

There was no inventory at the start of the year.

Selling price and costs

	Budget	Actual
	$	$
Selling price per unit	70	70
Variable costs per unit	55	55
Fixed production overhead	130,000	118,000
Fixed selling costs	75,000	75,000

Calculate the actual profit for the year that would be reported using marginal costing.

$ ☐☐☐☐ ('000)

2.3 **Which TWO of the following features distinguish throughput accounting from other costing systems?**

- ☐ Work in progress is valued at labour cost only.
- ☐ Work in progress is valued at material cost only.
- ☐ Costs are allocated to products when they are completed or sold.
- ☐ Only labour cost is treated as a variable cost.
- ☐ It does not attempt to maximise profit.

2.4 A company produces three products using three different machines. No other products are made on these particular machines. The following data is available for December 20X3:

	A	B	C
Contribution per unit	$36	$28	$18
Machine hours required per unit:			
Machine 1	5	2	1.5
Machine 2	5	5.5	1.5
Machine 3	2.5	1	0.5
Estimated sales demand (units)	50	50	60

Maximum machine capacity in December will be 400 hours per machine.

Calculate the machine utilisation rates for each machine for December 20X3 and identify which is the bottleneck machine(s).

- ☐ Machine 1
- ☐ Machine 2
- ☐ Machine 3
- ☐ Machines 1 and 2

2.5 WTD Co produces a single product. The management currently uses marginal costing but is considering using absorption costing in the future.

The budgeted fixed production overheads for the period are $500,000. The budgeted output for the period is 2,000 units. There were 800 units of opening inventory at the beginning of the period and 500 units of closing inventory at the end of the period.

If absorption costing principles were applied, the profit for the period compared to the marginal costing profit would be:

- ☐ $75,000 higher
- ☐ $75,000 lower
- ☐ $125,000 higher
- ☐ $125,000 lower

2.6 A manufacturing company recorded the following costs in October for Product X:

	$
Direct materials	20,000
Direct labour	6,300
Variable production overhead	4,700
Fixed production overhead	19,750
Variable selling costs	4,500
Fixed distribution costs	16,800
Total costs incurred for Product X	72,050

During October 4,000 units of Product X were produced but only 3,600 units were sold. At the beginning of October there was no inventory.

Using marginal costing, what was the value of inventory of Product X at the end of October?

- ☐ $3,080
- ☐ $3,100
- ☐ $3,550
- ☐ $5,075

2.7 If inventory levels have increased during the period, the profit calculated using marginal costing when compared with that calculated using absorption costing will be:

☐ Higher
☐ Lower
☐ Equal
☐ Impossible to answer without further information

2.8 One of the products manufactured by a company is Product J, which sells for $40 per unit and has a material cost of $10 per unit and a direct labour cost of $7 per unit. The total direct labour budget for the year is 50,000 hours of labour time at a cost of $12 per hour. Factory overheads are $2,920,000 per year.

The company is considering the introduction of a system of throughput accounting. It has identified that machine time is the bottleneck in the production process. Product J needs 0.01 hours of machine time per unit produced and the maximum capacity of the machine is 4,000 hours per year.

What is the throughput accounting ratio for Product J?

☐ 3.41
☐ 2.80
☐ 2.10
☐ 1.90

2.9 Last month a manufacturing company's profit was $2,000, calculated using absorption costing principles. If marginal costing principles had been used, a loss of $3,000 would have occurred. The company's fixed production cost is $2 per unit. Sales last month were 10,000 units.

What was last month's production (in units)?

☐ 7,500
☐ 9,500
☐ 10,500
☐ 12,500

2.10 Which of the following costing methods is most likely to produce useful information for decision-making?

☐ Marginal costing
☐ Activity based costing
☐ Total absorption costing
☐ Standard costing

2.11 PQ Co produces a single product. The budgeted fixed production overheads for the period are $400,000. The budgeted output for the period is 2,000 units. Opening inventory at the start of the period consisted of 1,800 units and closing inventory at the end of the period consisted of 900 units.

If absorption costing principles were applied, the profit for the period compared to the marginal costing profit would be:

☐ $540,000 higher
☐ $540,000 lower
☐ $180,000 higher
☐ $180,000 lower

2.12 JH Co produces three products, the L1, the L2 and the L3. The L1 has a TA ratio of 1.4, the L2 a ratio of 1.8, and the L3 has a ratio of 1.0.

Which of the following statements is true?

☐ L1 should be produced before L2.
☐ L3 should be produced before L1.
☐ L2 should be produced before L1.
☐ It is impossible to state a preference between the products.

2.13 M Co compares the profits reported under absorption costing and marginal costing during a period when the level of inventory has increased.

Which of the following statements is true?

☐ Absorption costing profits will be higher and closing inventory valuations lower than those under marginal costing

☐ Absorption costing profits will be higher and closing inventory valuations higher than those under marginal costing

☐ Marginal costing profits will be higher and closing inventory valuations lower than those under absorption costing

☐ Marginal costing profits will be higher and closing inventory valuations higher than those under absorption costing

2.14 J provides three different payroll services to businesses that cannot justify operating their own payroll departments. The following contribution and sales values have been determined for each of these services:

Service	X	Y	Z
Sales value per service ($)	100	200	100
Contribution per service ($)	40	70	25

If equal quantities of X, Y and Z are to be sold and fixed costs are $100,000 per month, the monthly sales value that would result in a profit of $40,000 is nearest to:

☐ $311,000
☐ $336,000
☐ $415,000
☐ $420,000

2.15 The following statements have been made about pricing:

(i) The mark up used in marginal costing is less arbitrary than the mark up used in full cost pricing.

(ii) The level of competition in the market is ignored under both full cost and marginal cost plus pricing.

(iii) The price elasticity of demand can be used to assess the impact on total revenue of changing the selling price of a product.

Which of the above statements are true?

☐ (i) and (ii)
☐ (ii) and (iii)
☐ (i) and (iii)
☐ (i), (ii) and (iii)

The following statements have been made about pricing:

(i)   When calculating a mark-up and a margin on the same product, the margin will be a higher percentage than the mark-up

(ii)   Using full cost pricing ensures that a product will generate a profit for the business

(iii) Marginal cost plus pricing is a form of relevant costing

Which of the above statements are true?

☐ (i) and (ii)
☐ (ii) and (iii)
☐ (i) and (iii)
☐ None of them

2.17 DF Co produces a single product and currently uses absorption costing for its internal management accounting reports. The fixed production overhead absorption rate is $46 per unit. Opening inventories for the year were 100 units and closing inventories were 210 units. The company's management accountant is considering a switch to marginal costing as the inventory valuation basis.

If marginal costing were used, the marginal costing profit for the year, compared with the profit calculated by absorption costing, would be which of the following?

☐ $5,060 lower
☐ $5,060 higher
☐ $4,600 lower
☐ $4,600 higher

3 Limiting factor analysis

3.1   Z Co manufactures three products, the selling price and cost details of which are given below:

	Product X	Product Y	Product Z
	$	$	$
Selling price per unit	75	95	96
Costs per unit:			
Direct materials ($5/kg)	10	5	15
Direct labour ($4/hour)	16	24	20
Variable overhead	8	12	10
Fixed overhead	24	36	30

In a period when direct materials are restricted in supply, the most and the least profitable uses of direct materials are:

	Most profitable	Least profitable
A	Y	X
B	Y	Z
C	Z	X
D	Z	Y

3.2 MNP plc produces three products from a single raw material that is limited in supply. Product details for period six are as follows:

	Product M	Product N	Product P
Maximum demand (units)	1,000	2,400	2,800
Optimum planned production	720	nil	2,800
Unit contribution	$4.50	$4.80	$2.95
Raw material cost per unit ($0.50 per kg)	$1.25	$1.50	$0.75

The planned production optimises the use of the 6,000 kg of raw material that is available from MNP plc's normal supplier at the price of $0.50 kg. However, a new supplier has been found that is prepared to supply a further 1,000 kg of the material.

Calculate the maximum price that MNP plc should be prepared to pay for the additional 1,000 kg of the material.

$ _____

3.3 **Which THREE of the following statements regarding marginal and absorption costing are true in the context of pricing decisions?**

☐ Marginal costing is appropriate for long-term pricing decisions.
☐ Marginal costing is appropriate for short-term pricing decisions.
☐ Absorption costing when used for pricing decisions includes the 'total-cost' of the product.
☐ Marginal costing ensures the recovery of all costs incurred in selling prices.
☐ Marginal costing is more appropriate than absorption costing for use in one-off pricing decisions.
☐ Absorption costing is more appropriate than marginal costing for use in one-off pricing decisions.

3.4 A company manufactures three products D, E and F. The company currently has a shortage of skilled labour, with total hours restricted to 5,400.

Details of these products are:

	D	E	F
Demand (units)	2,400	2,200	3,000
Contribution per unit	54	72	35
Skilled labour hours per unit	1	1.5	0.5

The mix of products that will maximise contribution is:

☐ (2,200 × E) + (2,100 × D)
☐ (1,000 × E) + (2,400 × D) + (3,000 × F)
☐ (2,200 × E) + (600 × D) + (3,000 × F)
☐ (2,400 × D) + (2,200 × E) + (3,000 × F)

3.5 The following data relates to Product W.

	Per unit
Selling price	$26.00
Material cost	$7.25
Labour cost	$5.75
Overhead cost	$5.00
Time on bottleneck resource	7 minutes

Using throughput accounting, the contribution per hour for Product W is:

☐ $68.57
☐ $106.75
☐ $130.71
☐ $160.71

3.6 HG plc manufactures four products. The unit cost, selling price and bottleneck resource details per unit are as follows.

	Product W	Product X	Product Y	Product Z
	$	$	$	$
Selling price	56	67	89	96
Material	22	31	38	46
Labour	15	20	18	24
Variable overhead	12	15	18	15
Fixed overhead	4	2	8	7
	Minutes	Minutes	Minutes	Minutes
Bottleneck resource time	10	10	15	15

If the company adopted throughput accounting and the products were ranked according to 'product return per minute', the highest ranked product would be:

☐ W

☐ X

☐ Y

☐ Z

3.7 The following budgeted data has been prepared for a company that manufactures four products:

Product	W	X	Y	Z
	$ per unit	$ per unit	$ per unit	$ per unit
Sales price	9.0	6.0	4.0	8.0
Variable cost	5.5	4.0	2.2	4.0
Budgeted sales units	20,000	25,000	50,000	12,500
Direct labour hours per unit	0.5	0.25	0.3	0.8

The total available direct labour hours in the period is 24,000 hours and the company plans to maximise profit.

Which is the correct ranking of products the company should make (highest to lowest)?

☐ X, W and Y

☐ W, X and Z

☐ W, Y and Z

☐ Y and Z only

3.8 A manufacturing company recorded the following costs in October for Product X:

	$
Direct materials	20,000
Direct labour	6,300
Variable production overhead	4,700
Fixed production overhead	19,750
Variable selling costs	4,500
Fixed distribution costs	16,800
Total costs incurred for Product X	72,050

During October 4,000 units of Product X were produced but only 3,600 units were sold. At the beginning of October there was no inventory.

The value of the inventory of Product X at the end of October using throughput accounting was:

☐ $630

☐ $1,080

☐ $1,100

☐ $2,000

3.9 In a time when labour supply is limited, a company has identified that it has 400 hours of labour available and that there is unlimited demand for each of its three products. Labour is paid $5 per hour.

	A	B	C
	$	$	$
Sales price per unit	20	23	25
Material cost per unit	3	2	4
Labour cost per unit	5	10	7.5

What is the optimal production plan?

☐ Produce 400 As
☐ Produce 200 Bs
☐ Produce 200 Cs
☐ Produce 200 As, 100 Bs and 200 Cs

3.10 Z plc manufactures three products which have the following selling prices and costs per unit:

	Z1	Z2	Z3
	$	$	$
Selling price	15.00	18.00	17.00
Costs per unit:			
Direct materials	4.00	5.00	10.00
Direct labour	2.00	4.00	1.80
Overhead:			
Variable	1.00	2.00	0.90
Fixed	4.50	3.00	1.35
	11.50	14.00	14.05
Profit per unit	3.50	4.00	2.95

All three products use the same type of labour.

In a period in which labour is in short supply, the rank order of production is:

	Z1	Z2	Z3
A	First	Second	Third
B	Third	Second	First
C	Second	First	Third
D	First	Third	Second

3.11 JR Co's accountant has correctly identified the scarce resource for the period is direct labour. He has calculated that the shadow price of direct labour is $4.50 per hour. Direct labour is currently paid $10 per hour.

If the objective of the company is to maximise profit in each period, how much should the company be willing to pay per hour to obtain additional direct labour hours of production capacity?

☐ Up to but not including $4.50
☐ Up to and including $4.50
☐ Up to but not including $14.50
☐ Up to and including $14.50

3.12 KP makes two products, the K and the P.

	K	P
	$	$
Selling price	160	98
Material C	20	0
Material D	20	20
Labour	60	40
Fixed costs per unit	15	10

Labour is in short supply and KP have only 21,000 hours available per month. Labour is paid $20 per hour.

What is the maximum contribution they can earn in the month?

$ [   ]

3.13 ABC Co makes three products, budget information is provided below.

	A	B	C
	$	$	$
Selling price	50	68	94
Material A	20	30	40
Material B	5	8	10
Labour	10	5	15
Demand (units)	1,000	2,000	3,000

Material A is in short supply and ABC Co only have 10,000 kg available. Material A costs $10 per kg.

What is the optimum production plan for ABC Co?

☐ 1000 As, 0 Bs and 2,975 Cs

☐ 0 As, 2,000 Bs and 3,000 Cs

☐ 1,000 As, 2,000 Bs and 500 Cs

☐ 1,000 As, 2,000 Bs and 3,000 Cs

3.14 **Are the following explanations of shadow prices true or false?**

	True	False
(i) The additional contribution generated from one additional unit of limiting factor.	☐	☐
(ii) The opportunity cost of not having the use of one extra unit of limiting factor.	☐	☐
(iii) The maximum amount that should be paid for one additional unit of scarce resource.	☐	☐

4 Relevant costs

4.1 S Co is considering adapting its assembly process so that products can also be moulded at the same time. The existing assembly process machinery would have to be removed, either now at a dismantling cost of $100,000 and with the sale of the machinery for $800,000, or in one year's time at a dismantling cost of $110,000 and with sale proceeds of $600,000. Alternative machinery would have to be leased. This would cost $80,000 per annum. The existing assembly process machinery originally cost $2,000,000 when purchased seven years ago. It is being depreciated at 5% per annum on a straight line basis.

Analysing on an incremental opportunity cost basis and ignoring the time value of money, which of the following is correct?

☐ Adapting now will produce savings of $130,000 more than adapting in one year.

☐ Adapting now will cost $130,000 more than adapting in one year.

☐ Adapting now will produce savings of $110,000 more than adapting in one year.

☐ Adapting now will cost $110,000 more than adapting in one year.

4.2 D Co's entire machine capacity is used to produce essential components. The variable costs of using the machines are $150,000 and the fixed costs are $400,000. If all the components were purchased from an outside supplier, the machines could be used to produce other items which would earn a total contribution of $250,000.

The maximum price that D Co should be willing to pay to the outside supplier for the components, assuming there is no change in fixed costs is:

$ [   ]

4.3 A special job for a customer will required 8 tonnes of a Material M. The company no longer uses this material regularly although it holds 3 tonnes in inventory. These originally cost $44 per tonne, and could be resold to a supplier for $35 per tonne. Alternatively these materials could be used to complete another job instead of using other materials that would cost $126 in total to purchase. The current market price of Material M is $50 per tonne. The company must decide whether to agree to the customer's request for the work, and to set a price.

What would be the relevant cost of Material M for this job?

☐ $250
☐ $355
☐ $376
☐ $400

4.4 **Which of the following are non-relevant costs?**

Select ALL that apply.

☐ Avoidable costs
☐ Opportunity costs
☐ Notional costs
☐ Sunk costs

4.5 A company is considering the use of material X in a special order. A sufficient quantity of the material, which is used regularly by the company in its normal business is available from inventory.

What is the relevant cost per kg of material X in the evaluation of the special order?

☐ Cost of the last purchase
☐ Nil
☐ Replacement cost
☐ Saleable value

4.6 CC Co is in the process of preparing a quotation for a special job for a customer. The job will require 510 units of material S. 420 units are already in stock at a book value of $50 per unit. The net realisable value per unit is $30. The replacement price per unit is $72. The material is in stock as a result of previous over buying. The units in stock could be used on another job as a substitute for 750 units of material V, which are about to be purchased at a price of $25 per unit.

The relevant cost of material S for this special job for the customer is:

$ [   ]

4.7 **Are the following statements about relevant costing true or false?**

	True	False
Sunk costs can never be a relevant cost for the purpose of decision-making.	☐	☐
If a company charges the minimum price for a product or service, based on relevant costs, it will not improve its overall profitability.	☐	☐

4.8 Sherburn plc has sufficient material Y in inventory for a year's production of 'stringfree'. Material Y cost $8,000 but is subject to major price variations; the current market price is double the original cost. It could be sold at the market price less 15% selling expenses. An alternative is to retain it for later use by which time the market price is expected to be $11,200.

The relevant cost of using material Y on the contract is:

$ [   ]

4.9 The following information is available for identifying the relevant cost of materials for a job for a customer. The company's management wants to establish a minimum price at which it is prepared to take on the job.

Material	Total quantity required	Currently in inventory	Carrying value per kg	Realisable value per kg	Replacement cost per kg
	kg	kg	$	$	$
X	500	300	5	3	7
Y	500	400	8	9	11
Z	100	100	10	12	15

Material Y is in regular use by the company. Materials X and Z are no longer in regular use.

What is the relevant cost of these materials for the job under consideration?

- ☐ $9,000
- ☐ $6,000
- ☐ $7,600
- ☐ $9,300

4.10 **What is the relevant cost of units of finished goods when disposing of them if they are no longer required?**

- ☐ Net realisable value
- ☐ Replacement cost
- ☐ Variable cost
- ☐ Full cost

4.11 **When analysing whether to replace an asset, which of the following is not relevant?**

- ☐ Balancing charge or allowance on the old asset
- ☐ Book value of the old asset
- ☐ Changes in working capital
- ☐ Removal costs of the old asset

4.12 X Co has 500 kg of material K in inventory for which it paid $2,000. The material is no longer in use in the company and could be sold for $1.50 per kg.

X Co is considering taking on a special order which will require 800 kg of material K. The current purchase price is $5 per kg.

In the assessment of the relevant cost of the decision to accept the special order, the cost of material K is:

- ☐ A sunk cost of $2,000
- ☐ A sunk cost of $2,000 and an incremental cost of $1,500
- ☐ An opportunity cost of $750 and an incremental cost of $1,500
- ☐ An incremental cost of $4,000.

---

5 Multi-product breakeven analysis

5.1 **Which TWO of the following options show how the breakeven point in units can be calculated?**

- ☐ Total fixed costs/contribution per unit
- ☐ Contribution required to break even/contribution per unit
- ☐ Contribution/sales
- ☐ Fixed costs/costs to sales ratio
- ☐ Contribution to sales ratio/contribution per unit

The following information is available for S Co.

	$'000
Revenue	1,000
Variable costs	600
Fixed costs	250
Profit	150

Assuming that the sales mix does not change, what increase in sales revenue would need to be achieved to increase the profit to $250,000?

- ☐ $150,000
- ☐ $400,000
- ☐ $100,000
- ☐ $250,000

5.3 A company provides three different levels of customer service support for one of its software products.

The following data relate to these three levels of support:

Support level	Superior	Standard	Basic
	$ per contract	$ per contract	$ per contract
Annual fee	1,000	750	400
Annual variable costs	450	250	170
Annual fixed costs (see note below)	200	100	50
Profit	350	400	180

Note: The total annual fixed costs are budgeted to be $1,200,000. None of these costs are specific to any type of customer service support.

Assume that the number of customer service support contracts sold are in the proportion:

Superior 20%   Standard 30%   Basic 50%

What is the annual revenue needed to break even?

(Give your answer to the nearest whole thousand)

$ ☐

5.4 A company makes and sells three products, R, S, and T. Extracts from the weekly profit statements are as follows.

	R	S	T	Total
	$	$	$	$
Sales	10,000	15,000	20,000	45,000
Variable cost of sales	4,000	9,000	10,000	23,000
Fixed costs*	3,000	3,000	3,000	9,000
Profit	3,000	3,000	7,000	13,000

*general fixed costs absorbed using a unit absorption rate

If the sales revenue mix of products produced and sold were to be changed to: R 20%, S 50%, T 30% then the new average contribution to sales ratio would be:

- ☐ Higher
- ☐ Lower
- ☐ Unchanged

5.5 A company sells three different levels of TV maintenance contract to its customers: Basic, Standard and Advanced. Selling prices, unit costs and monthly sales are as follows:

	Basic $	Standard $	Advanced $
Selling price	50	100	135
Variable cost	30	50	65
Monthly contracts sold	750	450	300

The average contribution to sales ratio of the company based on this sales mix is (to 1 decimal place):

[   ] %

5.6 A company makes and sells a single product. When sales per month are $6.8 million, total costs are $6.56 million. When sales per month are $5.2 million, total costs are $5.44 million. There is a step cost increase of $400,000 in fixed costs when sales are $6.0 million, but variable unit costs are constant at all levels of output and sales.

What is the breakeven point for sales revenue per month?

☐ $6.0 million
☐ There are two breakeven points: $5.64 million and $6.36 million
☐ $5.64 million only
☐ $6.36 million only

5.7 A company makes and sells three products. The budget for the next period is as follows:

	A $ per unit	B $ per unit	C $ per unit
Sales price	12	18	20
Variable cost	3	6	11
	9	12	9
Fixed cost	6	9	6
Profit	3	3	3
Number of units	30,000	40,000	10,000

What is the breakeven point in sales?

Give your answer in '000 to the nearest whole thousand.

$ [   ]

5.8 A company budgets to sells its three products A, B and C in the ratio 2:3:5 respectively, measured in units of sales. Unit sales prices and variable costs are as follows:

	A $ per unit	B $ per unit	C $ per unit
Sales price	20	18	24
Variable cost	11	12	18

Budgeted fixed costs are $1.2 million.

What sales will be needed to achieve a target profit of $400,000 for the period, to the nearest $1,000?

☐ $5.188 million
☐ $5.011 million
☐ $3.891 million
☐ $4.724 million

5.9 A company has fixed costs of $1.3 million. Variable costs are 55% of sales up to a sales level of $1.5 million, but at higher volumes of production and sales, the variable cost for incremental production units falls to 52% of sales.

What is the breakeven point in sales revenue?

Give your answer in '000 to the nearest whole thousand.

$ _____

5.10 A company makes and sells three products A, B and C. The products are sold in the proportions A: B: C = 1:1:4.

Monthly fixed costs are $55,100 and product details are as follows.

Product	Selling price $ per unit	Variable cost $ per unit
A	47	25
B	39	20
C	28	11

The company wishes to earn a profit of $43,000 next month.

The required sales value of product A in order to achieve this target profit is:

$ _____

5.11 F Scuttle Co has fixed costs of $50,000 per annum.

The company sells a single product for $25 per unit.

The contribution to sales ratio is 40%.

What is the breakeven point in revenue?

Breakeven point at $ _____

5.12 Blob Co has a budgeted breakeven sales revenue of $2 million and fixed costs of $800,000 for the month of June. The directors of Blob Co want to make a profit of $125,000.

What is the sales revenue that Blob Co needs to achieve?

☐ $2,800,000
☐ $3,000,000
☐ $2,312,500
☐ $2,125,000

5.13 A company provides a number of different services to its customers from a single office. The fixed costs of the office, including staff costs, are absorbed into the company's service costs using an absorption rate of $25 per consulting hour based on a budgeted activity level of 25,000 each quarter.

Fee income and variable costs are different depending on the services provided, but the average contribution to sales ratio is 35%. The breakeven annual fee income is closest to:

☐ $1,786,000
☐ $219,000
☐ $875,000
☐ $7,143,000

5.14 RDF Co offers four services to television companies The number of services provided is measured in service units and details of RDF Co's draft budget for its year ending 30 June 20X5 are as follows.

	Service K	Service L	Service M	Service N
Number of service units	1,000	2,300	1,450	1,970
Selling price per unit ($)	18	16	12	20
Variable cost per unit ($)	8	10	13	13
Fixed cost per unit ($)	2	3	2	4

The budgeted level of activity shown in the table above has been based on fully meeting the forecasted market demand for each type of service.

The following chart has been prepared based on the draft budget above.

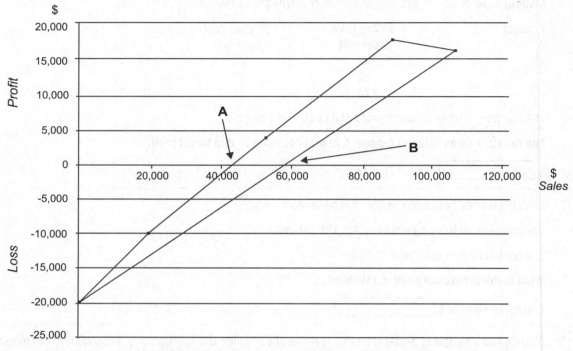

Choose options from the list below to correctly label points A and B of the multi product profit volume graph.

- Multi product break even point
- Break even point if services sold in the order K L N M
- Break even point if services sold in the order K M L N
- Break even point if services sold in the order L K M N

Point A: _____

Point B: _____

5.15 PER plc sells three products. The budgeted fixed cost for the period is $648,000. The budgeted contribution to sales ratio (C/S ratio) and sales mix are as follows

Product	C/S ratio	Mix
P	27%	30%
E	56%	20%
R	38%	50%

The breakeven revenue is:

Give your answer in '000 to the nearest whole thousand.

$ _____

5.16 Company X makes two products Y and Z, which it sells in the ratio 4:2. (This ratio is based on the sales revenue). The sales prices and variables costs of Y and Z are as follows:

	Sales price	Variable costs
Y	$61	$42
Z	$95	$63

Fixed costs for the business are $200,000.

The breakeven revenue for the business is closest to:

☐ $322,000
☐ $612,000
☐ $620,000
☐ $857,000

5.17 A company makes two different products in two different departments. Each department makes only one product.

Product A has a contribution to sales ratio of 0.7
Product B has a contribution to sales ratio of 0.74
Both are selling above their breakeven points

Based on the information provided which of the following statements is true?

☐ Variable costs in product A are 4% higher than in product B

☐ Product B will have a lower break-even point than product A

☐ The contribution earned by Product B grows more quickly than the contribution earned by product A as sales levels increase

☐ 70% of the selling price of product B contributes to fixed overheads and profits

---

5.18 T Co has prepared its budget for the next year, aiming to produce and sell 600,000 units. The following forecasts have also been made:

	$
Sales	500,000
Material costs	(90,000)
Labour costs	(80,000)
Variable overheads	(30,000)
Fixed overheads	(160,000)
Profit	140,000

For T Co's budget profit to reduce to zero, sales volume would have to change (as a percentage) by:

☐ 23%
☐ 27%
☐ 47%
☐ 50%

---

6 Short term decision making

6.1 L Co operates a process which produces three joint products: M, N and P. The costs of operating this process during control period 4 totalled $210,600. During the period the output of the three products was:

M 3,600 kg
N 8,100 kg
P 5,850 kg

N is further processed at a cost of $16.20 per kg. The actual loss in the second process was 10% of input, which is normal. Products M and P are sold without further processing.

The final selling prices of each product are:

M $36 per kg
N $32.40 per kg
P $45 per kg

Calculate the profit for Product N.

$ [   ]

6.2 HM Co has to decide whether to make component B in-house or to buy it from an external supplier. The costs to make component B are as follows:

	$
Variable cost	35,000
Fixed cost	50,000
	85,000

If component B is purchased from a supplier then other items could be produced instead which would earn a total contribution of $45,000

Calculate the maximum price that HM Co would be willing to pay to the supplier for component B.

$ [   ]

6.3 **If a company has to subcontract work to make up a shortfall in its own in-house capabilities, how will its total costs be minimised?**

☐ If those units bought from the subcontractor are the cheapest to buy.

☐ If those units bought from the subcontractor have the lowest extra variable cost per unit of scarce resource saved.

☐ If those units bought from the subcontractor have the highest extra variable cost per unit of scarce resource saved.

☐ If those units produced in house are the most expensive to produce.

6.4 **Which of the following is NOT a valid reason why the costs used for decision making may be different from the costs used for profit reporting?**

☐ Costs used for decision making include only costs that are affected by the decision

☐ Costs used for decision making never include fixed costs

☐ Costs used for decision making do not include past costs

☐ Costs used for decision making include opportunity costs

6.5 The performance of the three divisions of a company is detailed below:

	Division W	Division X	Division Y	Total
	$'000	$'000	$'000	$'000
Sales	700	840	300	1,840
Variable costs	560	420	240	1,220
Contribution	140	420	60	620
Fixed overheads				525
Net profit				95

40% of the fixed overheads are specific to the individual divisions. Each division incurs the same level of specific fixed overheads.

Which of the divisions should continue to operate if the company's objective is to maximise profits?

☐ All of divisions
☐ Division W and Division X only
☐ Division X only
☐ Division X and Division Y only

6.6 **Which of the following is an example of a feedback control?**

☐ Variance analysis
☐ Cash flow forecasting
☐ Forecasting future prices
☐ Budget setting process

6.7 **When deciding, purely on financial grounds, whether or not to process a joint product further, which THREE pieces of information are required?**

☐ The value of the common process costs
☐ The method of apportioning the common costs between the joint products
☐ The sales value of the joint product at the separation point
☐ The final sales value of the joint product
☐ The further processing cost of the joint product

6.8 **When deciding whether or not to further process a joint product after the separation point the information required is:**

Select ALL that apply.

☐ The costs of the joint process
☐ The costs of further processing
☐ The quantity of losses expected from further processing and their sales value
☐ The sales value prior to further processing
☐ The sales value after further processing
☐ The quantity of losses that occurred during the joint process and their sales value.

6.9 A manufacturing company has the following monthly budget.

	$	$
Sales		480,000
Direct materials	140,000	
Direct labour	110,000	
Variable overheads	50,000	
Fixed overheads	130,000	
Total costs		430,000
Profit		50,000

Sales can be increased by 15% per month if an extra work shift is added, but the sales price would have to be reduced by 3% on all units sold in order to sell the extra volume. Direct labour is a variable cost, but work in the extra shift would have to be paid an extra 50% per hour on top of the normal hourly rate. Increased materials purchase means that a 2% bulk purchase discount will be available on all material purchase. Additional fixed overheads would be $2,000 per month.

If the additional work shift is added, what will be the monthly profit?

- ☐ $51,400
- ☐ $52,150
- ☐ $53,410
- ☐ $60,060

6.10 In a manufacturing plant, the work force is operating at full capacity. The work force is paid a fixed rate of $12 per hour for a 35-hour week. This is a fixed weekly wage, although for the purpose of management accounting, direct labour costs are treated as a variable cost. A customer has asked for a special job to be done that would involve taking employees off regular work that earns a contribution of $15 per hour, after allowing for direct labour cost. The company must decide whether to agree to the customer's request for the work, and to set a price. The customers request is expected to take 10 hours.

What would be the relevant cost of labour for this job?

- ☐ $150
- ☐ $170
- ☐ $270
- ☐ $300

6.11 MM manufactures three components, S, A and T using the same machines for each and assembles them into a single product. The budget for the next year calls for the production and assembly of 4,000 of each component. The variable production cost per unit of the final product is as follows:

	Machine hours	Variable cost
		$
1 unit of S	3	20
1 unit of A	2	36
1 unit of T	4	24
Assembly		100

Only 24,000 hours of machine time will be available during the year, and a subcontractor has quoted the following unit prices for supplying components: S $29; A $40; T $34.

Using the options below each component, select MM's most profitable plan.

	S	A	T
Make			
	☐ 4,000	☐ 4,000	☐ 4,000
	☐ 3,000	☐ 3,000	☐ 3,000
	☐ 1,000	☐ 1,000	☐ 1,000
	☐ 0	☐ 0	☐ 0
Buy			
	☐ 4,000	☐ 4,000	☐ 4,000
	☐ 3,000	☐ 3,000	☐ 3,000
	☐ 1,000	☐ 1,000	☐ 1,000
	☐ 0	☐ 0	☐ 0

6.12 A company has received a special order which will require 1 kg each of material X, material Y and material Z. Information relating to each material is as follows:

	X	Y	Z
Cost per kg of material currently in inventory	$90	$60	$140
Current cost per kg	$100	$70	$150
Refund available per kg	$80	$nil	$100
Cost of disposal if not used	$nil	$30	$nil

Material X is used regularly, whereas, the company has no further use for material Y and Z. The company currently has more than 100 kg each of material X, Y and Z in stock.

Calculate the minimum price for materials X, Y and Z in the special order:

☐ $150
☐ $170
☐ $210
☐ $230

6.13 **Which of the following are disadvantages of choosing to outsource part of the production process to a third party?**

Select ALL that apply.

☐ Loss of control
☐ No access to expertise
☐ Increase in capital required
☐ Loss of competitive advantage
☐ Loss of capacity
☐ Loss of in-house skill

6.14 Lewis Co manufactures three products, K, L and G. Forecasted statements of profit or loss for next year are as follows:

	K	L	G	Total
	$'000s	$'000s	$'000s	$'000s
Sales	600	400	300	1,300
Cost of production				
Materials	(200)	(100)	(85)	(385)
Labour	(95)	(20)	(80)	(195)
Variable overhead	(75)	(10)	(20)	(105)
Fixed overhead	(250)	(120)	(80)	(450)
Gross margin	(20)	150	35	165
Selling costs	(30)	(20)	(50)	(100)
Net margin	(50)	130	(15)	65

Fixed production overheads consist of an apportionment of general factory overheads, based on 80% of direct materials cost. The remaining overheads are specific to the product concerned. Selling costs are based on commission paid to sales staff.

As profits are low the senior management are considering stopping production of one or more of the products.

Which product(s) should Lewis consider discontinuing?

☐ Product K
☐ Product G
☐ Product K & G
☐ No product should be discontinued

6.15 A company simultaneously produces three products (X, Y and Z) from a single process. X and Y are processed further before they can be sold. Z is a by-product that is sold immediately for $6 per unit without incurring any further costs. The sales prices of X and Y after further processing are $50 per unit and $60 per unit respectively. Data for October are as follows:

	$
Joint production costs that produced 2,500 units of X, 3,500 units of Y and 3,000 units of Z	140,000
Further processing costs for 2,500 units of X	24,000
Further processing costs for 3,500 units of Y	46,000

Joint costs are apportioned using the final sales value method.

Calculate the total cost of the production of X for October.

$ [   ]

6.16 A company is preparing a quotation for a one-off job that would require 1,200 kg of Material B. There are 900 kg of Material B in inventory that were bought at a cost of $3 per kg. The company does not foresee any other use for the material. The material held in inventory could be sold for $3.50 per kg. The current purchase price of Material B is $4.50 per kg.

The relevant cost of Material B to be included in the cost estimate is:

☐ $4,050
☐ $4,500
☐ $4,200
☐ $5,400

6.17 **A company makes three components, X, Y and Z. The costs to manufacture the components are as follows:**

	X	Y	Z
	$	$	$
Variable cost	5.00	16.00	10.00
Fixed cost	4.00	16.60	7.50
Total unit cost	9.00	32.60	17.50

The fixed costs are an allocation of general fixed overheads.

A supplier has offered to supply the components at the following prices:

Component X $8
Component Y $14
Component Z $11

Which components should the company buy in order to minimise total costs?

☐ Components X and Z
☐ Component Y only
☐ None of the components
☐ All of the components

6.18 **Which THREE of the following are categories of relevant costs?**

☐ Incremental costs
☐ Committed costs
☐ Sunk costs
☐ Differential costs
☐ Absorbed fixed costs
☐ Opportunity costs

7 Linear programming

7.1   A clothing company manufactures jackets and trousers.

The inputs for the two items are as follows:

	Jacket	Trousers
Cotton	3 m	2 m
Polyester	1.5 m	0.75 m
Labour	2 hours	1.5 hours

The maximum demand for jackets is 1,000, and for trousers 500 units. However, this does not include quantities ordered under a long term supermarket contract for 200 jackets and 50 pairs of trousers. The company would have to pay a substantial penalty if this were not satisfied.

All three resources are in short supply with maximum availability as follows:

Cotton 4,000 m, polyester 2,000 m, labour 2,800 hours.

There are not enough resources available to fulfil all of the demand and the contract units. In order to maximise contribution, the company is planning to use linear programming and needs to determine the constraints.

The constraint formula for cotton is:

- ☐ $3J + 2T \leq 3,300$
- ☐ $3J + 2T \leq 4,000$
- ☐ $3T + 2J \leq 4,700$
- ☐ $3T + 2J \leq 3,300$

7.2   **Which THREE of the following describe a shadow price?**

- ☐   The premium that should be paid for one additional unit of scarce resource
- ☐   The premium that should be paid for additional resources where there is no slack of that resource
- ☐   The minimum that should be paid for one additional unit of scarce resource
- ☐   The contribution that can be earned from one additional unit of scarce resource
- ☐   The total that should be paid for one extra unit of scarce resource

---

7.3   A company has demand for three products as follows:

A   500 units
B   200 units
C   100 units

The resource requirements are shown below:

	A	B	C
Labour hours	2	1	4
Material (l)	3	7	2

The resources are limited to labour hours of 1,600 and material 3,500 litres.

In determining the slack resources, which of the following is true?

- ☐   There is slack labour
- ☐   There is slack material
- ☐   There is slack labour and material
- ☐   Both material and labour have no slack

7.4   Tall and Short Co manufactures two types of chair, the T and the S. The following information is available.

	Chair T $ per unit	Chair S $ per unit
Selling price	130	145
Direct material	25	30
Direct labour	40	50
Variable overhead	20	30
Fixed overhead	10	5

If linear programming were used to calculate the optimum number of units to produce, which of the following would represent the iso-contribution line?

☐   C = 35T + 30S
☐   C = 45S + 35T
☐   C = 30S + 35T
☐   C = 45T + 35S

7.5   **In order to solve a product mix decision where multiple constraints exist, place the following in the correct order (1 to indicate first step, 2 to indicate second step etc) to show the methodology for determining the solution by the graphical method.**

Define the variables	☐
Plot a graph	☐
Identify feasible area	☐
Plot iso-contribution line	☐
Formulate constraints and objective function	☐
Determine optimal solution	☐

7.6   **Which of the following activities would form part of a linear programming analysis?**

Select ALL that apply.

☐   Identify the feasible area
☐   Identify the drivers of cost
☐   Allocate costs to cost pools
☐   Identify the breakeven point
☐   Formulate the constraints

7.7   A clothing company manufactures jackets and trousers.

The inputs for the two items are as follows:

	Jacket	Trousers
Cotton	3 m	2 m
Polyester	1.5 m	0.75 m
Labour	2 hours	1.5 hours

The maximum demand for jackets is 1,000, and for trousers 500 units. However, this does not include quantities ordered under a long term supermarket contract for 200 jackets and 50 pairs of trousers. The company would have to pay a substantial penalty if this were not satisfied.

All three resources are in short supply with maximum availability as follows:

Cotton 4,000 m, polyester 2,000 m, labour 2,800 hours.

There are not enough resources available to fulfil all of the demand and the contract units. In order to maximise contribution, the company is planning to use linear programming and needs to determine the constraints:

The constraint formula for labour is:

- ☐ $2J + 1.5T \leq 2,325$
- ☐ $2J + 1.5T \leq 2,800$
- ☐ $2J + 1.5T \leq 3,275$
- ☐ $1.5J + 2T \leq 2,325$

7.8   A company produces two products, the Wang and the Tang using the same resources. The company is determining the production plan for the period in the face of multiple resource constraints. Using linear programming it has been established that, at the point at which contribution is maximised, there are two resources used by the company that are binding constraints.

The binding constraints are formulated as follows where W and T represent the units of each product that can be produced:

Labour $4W + 2T \leq 12,500$
Machine hours $3W + 4T \leq 15,000$

The number of units of Product Tang that can be produced under the optimal production plan is:

	units.

7.9   **Complete the following using the words below:**

BINDING
MAXIMUM
MINIMUM
CRITICAL
DETERMINANTS

Slack occurs when the [＿＿＿＿＿＿＿＿] availability of a resource is not used in the optimal solution.

Surplus occurs when there is production excess of a [＿＿＿＿＿＿＿＿] requirement. If there is no slack then the constraints are said to be [＿＿＿＿＿＿＿＿].

7.10   B plc manufactures two types of boots, Knee High (K) and Ankle High (A). The following information is available:

	Knee High $ per unit	Ankle High $ per unit
Selling price	40	30
Direct material	8	4
Direct labour	7	5
Variable overhead	8	6
Fixed overhead	11	8

If linear programming were used to calculate the optimum number of units to produce which of the following would represent the iso-contribution line?

- ☐ $C = 15K + 17A$
- ☐ $C = 6K + 7A$
- ☐ $C = 17K + 15A$
- ☐ $C = 7K + 6A$

7.11 Product A sells for $140.

The cost card is:

	$
Material X 2 m at $3 per metre	6
Material Y 3 m at $8 per metre	24
Labour 3 hrs at $15	45
Fixed overhead 3 hrs at 10	30

Material X in short supply and there is not enough to meet maximum demand. Material Y is not in short supply.

Complete the following:

The shadow price for material X is: $ [   ] per metre.

7.12 Product A sells for $140.

The cost card is:

	$
Material X 2 m at $3 per metre	6
Material Y 3 m at $8 per metre	24
Labour 3 hrs at $15	45
Fixed overhead 3 hrs at 10	30

Material X in short supply and there is not enough to meet maximum demand. Material Y is not in short supply.

Complete the following:

The shadow price for Material Y is: $ [   ] per metre

7.13 **Which of the following are assumptions of linear programming?**

Select all that apply:

- ☐ Units of output are not divisible
- ☐ Total amount of scarce resource is known with certainty
- ☐ Fixed costs are unchanged by the decision
- ☐ There is no interdependence of demand between products
- ☐ Unit variable cost is constant

7.14 A clothing company manufactures jackets and trousers.

The inputs for the two items are as follows:

	Jacket	Trousers
Cotton	3 m	2 m
Polyester	1.5 m	0.75 m
Labour	2 hours	1.5 hours

The maximum demand for jackets is 1,000, and for trousers 500 units. However, this does not include quantities ordered under a long term supermarket contract for 200 jackets and 50 pairs of trousers. The company would have to pay a substantial penalty if this were not satisfied.

All three resources are in short supply with maximum availability as follows:

Cotton 4,000 m, polyester 2,000 m, labour 2,800 hours.

There are not enough resources available to fulfil all of the demand and the contract units. In order to maximise contribution, the company are planning to use linear programming and needs to determine the constraints.

The constraint formula for polyester is:

☐ $1.5J + 0.75T \leq 1{,}662.5$
☐ $1.5J + 0.75T \leq 2{,}000$
☐ $1.5J + 0.75T \leq 2{,}337.5$
☐ $0.75J + 1.5T \leq 1{,}662.5$

7.15 A European directive has decreed that all companies should make more foods deemed to be 'healthy' than those deemed to be 'not healthy'.

Which of the following correctly represents the constraint line to represent this directive on a graphical linear programming solution, where H = healthy and N = not healthy?

☐ $N - H < 0$
☐ $N + H = 0$
☐ $H - N < 0$
☐ $N - H > 0$

7.16 A solution to a graphical linear programming problem showed that the optimal solution was found at the intersection of two constraint lines determined by the following set of simultaneous equations:

- $6x + 4y = 5{,}800$
- $14x - 10y = 5{,}800$

Complete the following:

The optimal number of product X =

The optimal number of product Y =

8 Risk and uncertainty in decision making

8.1 The owner of a van selling hot take-away food has to decide how many burgers to purchase for sale at a forthcoming outdoor concert. The number of burgers sold will depend on the weather conditions and any unsold burgers will be thrown away at the end of the day.

The table below details the profit that would be earned for each possible outcome:

Weather	Number of burgers purchased			
	1,000	2,000	3,000	4,000
Bad	$1,000	$0	($1,000)	($3,000)
Average	$3,000	$6,000	$7,000	$6,000
Good	$3,000	$6,000	$9,000	$12,000

If the van owner applies the maximin rule he will purchase:

☐ 1,000 burgers
☐ 2,000 burgers
☐ 3,000 burgers
☐ 4,000 burgers

8.2 The owner of a van selling hot take-away food has to decide how many burgers to purchase for sale at a forthcoming outdoor concert. The number of burgers sold will depend on the weather conditions and any unsold burgers will be thrown away at the end of the day.

The table below details the profit that would be earned for each possible outcome:

Weather	Number of burgers purchased			
	1,000	2,000	3,000	4,000
Bad	$1,000	$0	($1,000)	($3,000)
Average	$3,000	$6,000	$7,000	$6,000
Good	$3,000	$6,000	$9,000	$12,000

If the van owner applies the minimax regret rule he will purchase:

☐ 1,000 burgers
☐ 2,000 burgers
☐ 3,000 burgers
☐ 4,000 burgers

8.3 A company is considering whether to develop and market a new product.

The cost of developing the product is estimated to be $100,000. There is a 70% probability that the development will succeed and a 30% probability that it will be unsuccessful, and the development costs will be lost.

If the development succeeds then the product will be marketed.

- There is a 50% chance that the marketing will be very successful and that profits of $150,000 will be made.

- There is a 40% chance that the marketing will be moderately successful and that profits of $50,000 will be made.

- There is a 10% chance that the marketing will be unsuccessful and that losses of $120,000 will be made.

The profit and loss figures take into account the development costs of $100,000.

The expected value of the decision to develop and market the product is:

☐ $83,000
☐ ($17,000)
☐ $58,100
☐ $28,100

8.4 A company can choose from three mutually exclusive projects. The net cash flows from the projects will depend on market demand. All of the projects will last only for one year. The forecast net cash flows, their associated probabilities and the expected values of the projects are given below.

Market demand	Weak	Average	Good	Expected value
Probability	0.40	0.30	0.30	1.00
Net cash flows	$'000s	$'000s	$'000s	$'000s
Project A	400	500	600	490
Project B	300	350	640	417
Project C	450	480	500	474

The maximum amount that should be paid for perfect information regarding market demand is:

$ ☐☐☐☐☐☐ 000

8.5 **A risk neutral decision maker will:**

☐ Ignore risk entirely in decision making
☐ Ignore risk when making decisions between projects that deliver the same expected value
☐ Avoid risk by trying to neutralise its impact
☐ Seek risk, because they are indifferent to risk

8.6 Nile Co is preparing its sales budget for 20X4. The sales manager estimates that sales will be 120,000 units if the summer is rainy, and 80,000 units if the summer is dry. The probability of a dry summer is 0.4.

What is the expected value for sales volume for 20X4?

☐ 96,000 units
☐ 100,000 units
☐ 104,000 units
☐ 120,000 units

8.7 The probability of an expected profit of $2,000 is 0.34, the probability of an expected profit of $1,850 is 0.15, the probability of an expected profit of $1,000 is 0.3 and the probability of an expected loss of $3,000 is 0.21.

What is the probability of a profit of $1,000 or less?

☐ 0.21
☐ 0.3
☐ 0.49
☐ 0.51

8.8 P Co currently sells 90,000 units of product Y per annum. At this level of sales and output, the selling price and variable cost per unit are $50 and $21 respectively. The annual fixed costs are $1,200,000. The management team is considering lowering the selling price per unit to $45.

The estimated levels of demand at the new price, and the probabilities of them occurring, are:

Selling price of $45

Demand	Probability
100,000 units	0.45
120,000 units	0.55

It is thought that at either of the higher sales and production levels, the variable cost per unit, and the probability of it occurring, will be as follows:

Variable cost (per unit)	Probability
$20	0.40
$18	0.60

Calculate the probability that lowering the selling price to $45 per unit would increase profit.

[   ]

8.9 A company expects to sell 1,000 units per month of a new product but there is uncertainty as to both the unit selling price and the unit variable cost of the product. The following estimates of selling price, variable costs and their related probabilities have been made:

Selling price $ per unit	Probability %	Unit variable cost $ per unit	Probability %
20	25	8	20
25	40	10	50
30	35	12	30

There are specific fixed costs of $5,000 per month expected for the new product. The probability of monthly contribution from this new product exceeding $13,500 is:

☐ 24.5%

☐ 30.5%

☐ 63.0%

☐ 92.5%

8.10 D provides a motorist rescue service to its members. It has been proposed to change the annual membership fee to $120 for the next year. The impact of this on the number of members is uncertain but the following estimates have been made:

Number of members	Probability
20,000	0.1
30,000	0.6
40,000	0.3

It is thought that the variable operating costs vary in relation to the number of members but the cost per member is uncertain. The following estimates have been made:

Variable cost per member	Probability
$70	0.3
$60	0.5
$40	0.2

D expects to incur annual fixed costs of $1,100,000.

The management accountant of D has produced a two-way data table.

Calculate the value that would be shown in that table in the cell for the profit from 40,000 members with a variable cost per member of $40.

$ ▭

8.11 The following decision tree shows four decision options: 1, 2, 3 and 4.

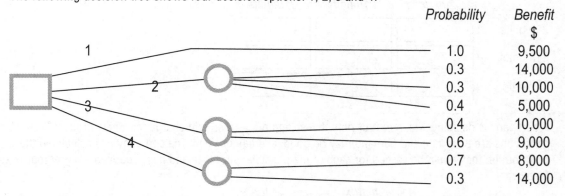

	Probability	Benefit $
1	1.0	9,500
2	0.3	14,000
	0.3	10,000
	0.4	5,000
	0.4	10,000
3	0.6	9,000
4	0.7	8,000
	0.3	14,000

Using the expected value rule, which choice should be made so as to optimise the expected benefit?

☐ Choice 1
☐ Choice 2
☐ Choice 3
☐ Choice 4

8.12 A manager is deciding which of four potential selling prices to choose for a new product.

The estimated contribution depending on combination of selling price and demand is shown in the payoff table below:

Selling price	$60	$70	$80	$90

Demand level

	$'000	$'000	$'000	$'000
Excellent	50	60	40	30
Good	40	50	30	20
Weak	20	35	20	10

If the manager applies the maximin criterion to make decisions, the selling price chosen would be:

☐ $60
☐ $70
☐ $80
☐ $90

8.13 A company has produced a payoff table showing the profit earned depending on a combination of the production and demand.

Payoff table	Units produced		
	200 units	210 units	220 units
Demand			
200 units	$12,000	$11,600	$11,200
210 units	$12,000	$12,600	$12,200
220 units	$12,000	$12,600	$13,200

Complete the minimax regret table using the list of numbers below.

$0
$400
$600
$800
$1,200

Payoff table	Units produced		
	200 units	210 units	220 units
200 units			
210 units			
220 units			

8.14 A company is deciding which of four potential selling prices it should charge for a new product. Market conditions are uncertain and demand may be good, average or poor. The company has calculated the contribution that would be earned for each of the possible outcomes and has produced a regret matrix as follows:

Regret matrix

Demand level	Selling price			
	$140	$160	$180	$200
Good	$20,000	$60,000	$0	$10,000
Average	$50,000	$0	$40,000	$20,000
Poor	$0	$30,000	$20,000	$30,000

If the company applies the minimax regret criterion to make decisions, which selling price would be chosen?

☐ $140
☐ $160
☐ $180
☐ $200

8.15 **Are the following statements about decision trees true or false?**

	True	False
A decision tree can be used to identify the preferred decision choice using the minimax regret decision rule.	☐	☐
A decision tree is likely to present a simplified representation of reality.	☐	☐

8.16 You are asked to interpret the following extract from a decision tree, which has been prepared for a decision that is to be made to choose between A, B and C.

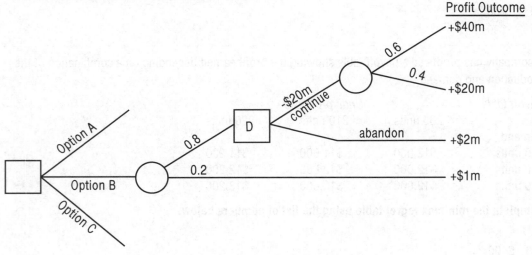

What is the maximum expected value of profit at decision point D?

☐ $12 million
☐ $14 million
☐ $32 million
☐ $9.8 million

8.17 **A decision maker using the maximin decision criteria will:**

☐ Assume that they can ignore risk and will choose the outcome with the highest expected value.

☐ Assume that they will regret not having chosen another alternative and will therefore minimise the possible loss under this assumption.

☐ Assume that the worst outcome will always occur and will select the largest payoff under this assumption.

☐ Assume that the best payoff will always occur and will select the option with the largest payoff.

8.18 A company is considering the costs of a new product. The following table shows the predictions made for fixed costs and variable costs together with their associated probabilities for a particular output quantity.

Fixed costs ($)	Probability
100,000	0.40
120,000	0.35
150,000	0.25

Variable costs ($)	Probability
80,000	0.35
100,000	0.45
140,000	0.20

The expected value for the particular output order quantity is: $ [_____]

8.19 A production manager has determined that when the equipment is working properly, the mean weight of items coming off a production line is 80 kg. The standard deviation is 5 kg.

An item has just been taken from the production line at random and weighs 84 kg.

What is the percentage chance (to two decimal places) that an item would weigh 84 kg or more when the equipment is working correctly?

[_____] %

8.20 **Which investment would a risk averse investor choose?**

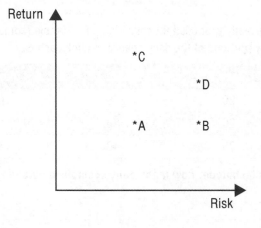

☐ Project A
☐ Project B
☐ Project C
☐ Project D

8.21 A supplier will supply company A in batches of 100 units, but daily demand is unpredictable. Company A has prepared a payoff table to reflect the expected profits if different quantities are purchased and in differing market demand conditions.

Market conditions	Probability	Purchase 100	Purchase 200	Purchase 300	Purchase 400
Weak	15%	50	(100)	(200)	(250)
Average	25%	120	120	250	100
Strong	50%	90	200	300	400
Exceptional	10%	80	300	400	500

If the maximin criteria is applied, how many units would be purchased from the supplier?

☐ 100
☐ 200
☐ 300
☐ 400

8.22 A supplier will supply company B in batches of 100 units, but daily demand is unpredictable. Company B has prepared a payoff table to reflect the expected profits if different quantities are purchased and in differing market demand conditions.

Market conditions	Probability	Purchase 100	Purchase 200	Purchase 300	Purchase 400
Weak	15%	50	(100)	(200)	(250)
Average	25%	120	120	250	100
Strong	50%	90	200	300	400
Exceptional	10%	80	300	400	500

If the maximax criteria is applied, how many units would be purchased from the supplier?

☐ 100
☐ 200
☐ 300
☐ 400

8.23 A restaurant owner has correctly produced the following pay off table (containing total contribution values) for their decision of how many portions of the daily special to cook each day:

Demand	Make 5	Make 10	Make 15	Make 20
Poor	20	(10)	(5)	(20)
Average	20	30	35	40
Strong	20	40	45	50

Using the minimax regret technique, how many daily specials should the restaurant cook?

[   ]

8.24 JB Co is launching a new product and there is uncertainty surrounding the level of fixed and variable costs. The following table shows the predictions made for fixed costs and variable costs together with their associated probabilities if 10,000 units are manufactured and sold for $70 each.

Fixed costs ($)	Probability
20,000	0.40
30,000	0.35
40,000	0.25

Variable cost per unit ($)	Probability
60	0.35
55	0.45
50	0.20

The expected value of the contribution for 10,000 is: $ [   ]

8.25 You are asked to interpret the following extract from a decision tree, which has been prepared for a decision that is to be made to choose between A, B and C.

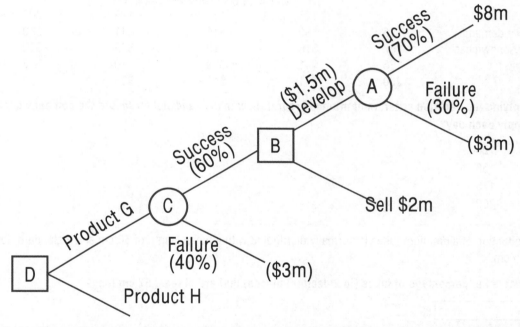

What is the maximum expected value of profit at decision point B? Provide your answer in $m and round to one decimal place).

$ [   ]

8.26 A risk neutral investor has prepared the following table of profits to use when choosing between three investments.

Investment	Good economic conditions $m	Average economic conditions $m	Bad economic conditions $m
1	20	20	20
2	40	30	0
3	5	25	30

The probability of good economic conditions is 30%, average 50% and bad conditions is 20%.

What is the maximum the investor would be prepared to pay for a market research survey which could correctly predict the economic conditions?

$ [   ] m

8.27 Bread Co has decided to start selling sandwiches which it will deliver to local offices daily. Demand is expected to vary between 125 and 200 sandwiches each day. As the day progresses, the price of the sandwiches is reduced and at the end of the day, sandwiches which have not been sold are thrown away. The company has prepared a regret table to show the amount of profit which would be foregone each day at each of the four possible supply levels.

		Daily supply of sandwiches (units) 125	150	175	200
Daily demand	125	$0	$11	$41	$60
for sandwiches	150	$18	$0	$22	$39
(units)	175	$41	$20	$0	$17
	200	$71	$45	$26	$0

Applying the decision criterion of minimax regret, how many sandwiches should the company decide to supply each day?

☐ 125
☐ 150
☐ 175
☐ 200

8.28 Production of aluminium tubes is normally distributed with a mean length of 50 cm and a standard deviation of 5 cm.

What is the percentage of tubes (to 2 decimal places) that are at least 57 cm long?

[   ] %

9 Forecasting techniques

9.1 **Which of the following components of a time series would be identified as a cyclical variation?**

☐ Occasional peaks which occur unpredictably but on average once every five years.

☐ Regular cycles involving an increase in the first half of each year, followed by a corresponding decrease in the second half of the year.

☐ A peak in the first three years of every decade, with a corresponding trough in the last five years of every decade.

☐ An increase of the same amount each year over the last 50 years.

9.2 BF Co manufactures a single product, and an extract from the flexed budget for production costs is as follows.

	Activity level	
	80%	90%
	$	$
Direct material	3,200	3,600
Direct labour	2,800	2,900
Production overhead	5,400	5,800
	11,400	12,300

The total production cost in a budget that is flexed at the 88% level of activity is:

$ [   ]

9.3 **For the linear equation y = a + bx, which THREE of the following variable definitions are correct?**

☐ y is the independent variable, whose value helps to determine the corresponding value of x.
☐ x is the dependent variable, depending for its value on the value of y.
☐ a is a constant, a fixed amount.
☐ x is the independent variable, whose value helps to determine the corresponding value of y.
☐ y is the dependent variable, depending for its value on the value of x.

9.4 For some quarterly sales data, the trend has been calculated as increasing by 6 each quarter and the average seasonal variation for the third quarter as - 22.5. The most recent data available is for the second quarter of Year 3 when sales were 370 units, and a centred moving average for the fourth quarter of Year 2 was 330.625 units.

Using the additive model, predicted sales for the third quarter of Year 3 are?

☐ 376 units
☐ 349 units
☐ 308 units
☐ 326 units

9.5 The regression equation Y = 53X − 258 has been determined as a reliable estimate of Mac Co's deseasonalised sales (Y) in units for a control period X. Quarterly seasonal variations affecting Mac Co's sales levels are as follows.

Q1	Q2	Q3	Q4
−20%	−30%	+5%	+45%

The forecast sales level to the nearest whole unit for control period 17, which is in quarter 3 is:

[   ] units

9.6 Z plc has found that it can estimate future sales using time-series analysis and regression techniques. The following trend equation has been derived:

y = 25,000 + 6,500x

Where

y is the total number of units per quarter, and

x is the time period reference number.

Z has also derived the following set of seasonal variation index values for each quarter using a multiplicative (proportional) model:

Quarter 1	70
Quarter 2	90
Quarter 3	150
Quarter 4	90

Using the above model, the forecast for sales units for the third quarter of year 7, assuming that the first quarter of year 1 is time period reference number 1 is:

☐ units

9.7 The following extract is taken from the production cost budget for K Co.

| Production (units) | 1,650 | 2,400 |
| Production cost | $20,770 | $23,170 |

The budget cost allowance for an activity level of 1,980 units is:

$ ☐

9.8 A shop has recorded its sales for the last 2½ years as:

Year	Quarter	Sales
1	1	300
	2	320
	3	275
	4	280
2	5	340
	6	355
	7	300
	8	300
3	9	360
	10	370

Using a centred annual moving average, the trend figure for the first quarter of year 2 is predicted as:

☐ 317.50
☐ 315.63
☐ 340.00
☐ 312.50

9.9 **The definition of a trend is:**

☐ A medium-term change in results caused by circumstances which repeat in cycles.
☐ An underlying long-term movement over time in the values of the data recorded.
☐ A short-term fluctuation due to different circumstances which affect results at different points in time.
☐ A non-recurring fluctuation caused by unforeseen circumstances.

9.10 A sales analyst has established the following trend figures and seasonal variations for a company's sales:

Quarter	1	2	3	4
	$'000	$'000	$'000	$'000
Year 7	1,500	1,528	1,552	1,530
Year 8	1,557	1,580	1,608	1,632
Average seasonal variation	−18	+3	+29	−14

The analyst forecasts that the trend will increase by $25,000 per quarter in years 9 and 10.

What is the forecast sales value for the first quarter of year 10 ($'000)?

☐ 1,757
☐ 1,775
☐ 1,714
☐ 1,739

9.11 **When a moving average is plotted onto a graph, where should the plotted points be located?**

☐ At the end of the period to which they apply
☐ At the beginning of the period to which they apply
☐ At the mid-point of the period to which they apply
☐ Anywhere

9.12 By linear regression, the relationship between the monthly quantity produced (x) and total production cost (y) was found to be $y = 15,000 + 286x$.

Estimate the variable production cost if output is 400 units.

☐ $114,400
☐ $100,000
☐ $129,400
☐ $14,400

9.13 The following extract is taken from the production cost budget of L plc:

Output	2,000 units	3,500 units
Total cost	$12,000	$16,200

The budget cost allowance for an output of 4,000 units would be:

☐ $17,600
☐ $18,514
☐ $20,400
☐ $24,000

9.14 Bing Co has the following cost information:

	Month 1	Month 2
Production (units)	250	300
Costs ($)	2,750	3,390
Index	110	113

All of the costs are variable.

The monthly cost predicted for month 3 when production is anticipated to be 350 units and the index is predicted to be 114 is

$ ▢

9.15 **Which of the following activities will be made possible if a company uses regression analysis to determine the trend of production costs?**

☐ Prediction of future costs for any future level of activity
☐ Analysis of past deviations from budgeted costs
☐ Prediction of future costs for activity levels within the company's relevant range
☐ Identification of the cause of an increase in costs

9.16 K Co has used regression analysis to determine the relationship between production costs and labour hours in its factory. The solution was determined as: $y = 18,000 + 3x$

Where

y = total monthly production cost
x = number of labour hours per month

In 20X7 production in January is expected to use 15,000 labour hours. After that, production levels will rise at a steady rate of 4% per month for the next two months, before stabilising for the remainder of the year.

What are the expected production costs for the year 20X7?

$ ▢

10 Budgeting for planning

10.1 What is another name for tactical planning?

- ☐ Strategic planning
- ☐ Budgetary planning
- ☐ Operation planning
- ☐ Corporate planning

10.2 Which of the following are functional budgets?

Select all that apply.

- ☐ Purchasing budget
- ☐ Cash budget
- ☐ Sales budget
- ☐ Marketing cost budget

10.3 BDL plc is currently preparing its cash budget for the year to 31 March 20X8. An extract from its sales budget for the same year shows the following sales values.

	$
March	60,000
April	70,000
May	55,000
June	65,000

40% of its sales are expected to be for cash. Of its credit sales, 70% are expected to pay in the month after sale and take a 2% discount. 27% are expected to pay in the second month after the sale, and the remaining 3% are expected to be bad debts.

The value of sales receipts to be shown in the cash budget for May 20X7 is:

$ [   ]

10.4 Which of the following definitions describe 'zero-based budgeting'?

Select all that apply.

- ☐ A method of budgeting where an attempt is made to make the expenditure under each cost heading as close to zero as possible.

- ☐ Zero-based budgeting is a method of budgeting whereby all activities are re-evaluated each time a budget is formatted.

- ☐ A method of budgeting that recognises the difference between the behaviour of fixed and variable costs with respect to changes in output and the budget is designed to change appropriately with such fluctuations.

- ☐ A method of budgeting where the sum of revenues and expenditures in each budget centre must equal zero.

10.5 When preparing a material purchases budget, what is the quantity to be purchased?

- ☐ Materials required for production – opening inventory of materials – closing inventory of materials
- ☐ Materials required for production – opening inventory of materials + closing inventory of materials
- ☐ Opening inventory of materials – materials required for production – closing inventory of materials
- ☐ Opening inventory of materials + closing inventory of materials – materials required for production

10.6 **Of what does the master budget comprise?**

Select ALL that apply.

☐ The budgeted statement of profit or loss

☐ The budgeted statement of cash flow, budgeted statement of profit or loss and budgeted statement of financial position

☐ The entire set of budgets prepared

☐ The budgeted cash flow

10.7 **Which of the following could be used to describe activity based budgeting?**

Select all that apply.

☐ A method of budgeting based on an activity framework and utilising cost driver data in the budget-setting and variance feedback processes

☐ The use of costs determined using ABC as a basis for preparing budgets

☐ The definition of the activities that underlie the financial figures in each function and the use of the level of activity to decide how much resource should be allocated, how well it is being managed and to explain variances from budget

---

10.8 **Which of the following is NOT a common criticism of incremental budgeting?**

☐ It assumes that all current activities and costs are still needed.
☐ There is no requirement for managers to justify existing costs.
☐ There is no incentive for managers to reduce costs.
☐ There are no performance targets for managers.

10.9 D plc operates a retail business. Purchases are sold at cost plus 25%. The management team are preparing the cash budget and have gathered the following data:

1 The budgeted sales are as follows:

Month	$
July	100
August	90
September	125
October	140

2 It is management policy to hold inventory at the end of each month which is sufficient to meet sales demand in the next half month. Sales are budgeted to occur evenly during each month.

3 Payables are paid one month after the purchase has been made.

What is the entry for 'purchases' that will be shown in the cash budget for September?

[   ]

10.10 **Put the following stages of an activity based budgeting system in chronological order.**

- 1st
- 2nd
- 3rd
- 4th

A Take action to adjust the capacity of resources to match the projected supply [   ]

B Determine the resources that are required to perform organisation activities [   ]

C Estimate the production and sales volume by individual products and customers [   ]

D Estimate the demand for organisational activities [   ]

10.11 **Are the following statements about rolling budgets true or false?**

	True	False
Rolling budgets may be used to alter plans instead of encouraging managers to focus on improving performance.	☐	☐
Rolling budgets are not worth preparing unless there is a persistent and large amount of uncertainty about the future.	☐	☐

10.12 **Which of the following weaknesses in a budgeting system is most likely to be found in a top-down system of budgeting?**

☐ Management budgets may include excessive amounts of 'slack' (unnecessary budget spending allowances)

☐ Management budgets may be too ambitious and beyond the realistic resource capabilities of the organisation

☐ Management budgets may not be realistic in practice

☐ Budgets may be inconsistent with the long-term strategy of the organisation

10.13 **For which of the following reasons is budgeting more difficult in public sector organisations (such as government and the police force) than in private sector companies?**

Select all that apply.

☐ Difficulty in quantifying objectives
☐ Spending limits imposed by government
☐ Difficulty in quantifying outputs
☐ The public sector is larger than the private sector

10.14 The following details have been taken from the receivables collection records of W plc:

Invoices paid in the month after sale	60%
Invoices paid in the second month after sale	20%
Invoices paid in the third month after sale	15%
Bad debts	5%

Customers paying in the month after the sale are allowed a 10% discount.

Invoices for sales are issued on the last day of the month in which the sales are made.

The budgeted credit sales for the final five months of this year are:

Month	August	September	October	November	December
Credit sales	$80,000	$100,000	$120,000	$130,000	$160,000

The total amount budgeted to be received in December from credit sales is:

$ ☐

10.15 Oboe Co is preparing its budgets for the next month.

It has calculated that it needs to produce 11,875 units of finished product C, each of which required 4 labour hours to complete. There is unavoidable idle time in the factory due to production changeovers and it is currently running at 5%. The basic hourly rate for labour is $12. However if labour exceeds 40,000 hours in any one month this will be paid at time and a half.

Calculate the labour budget, in $ for the period.

☐ $598,500
☐ $600,000
☐ $657,750
☐ $660,000

10.16 Bag Co has sales values for the first four months of the year as follows:

Jan $12,000
Feb $16,000
Mar $17,000
Apr $18,000

It is preparing its cash budgets and has noted the following past pattern of behaviour from customers:

20% of customers pay in cash at the time of the sale

50% of customers pay in the month after the sale, having been given a 1% discount to encourage prompt payment

15% of customers pay 2 months after the sale

10% of customers pay 3 months after the sale

5% of sales are written off as bad debts.

Calculate the budgeted sales receipts for April.

- ☐ $15,615
- ☐ $15,700
- ☐ $16,215
- ☐ $17,010

10.17 **Match the budgeting terms provided to the definitions below:**

| | does not affect the optimal solution in a linear programming solution |

| | is altered to reflect the actual level of activity |

| | constrains what the business can achieve in the budget period |

Picklist:

A bottleneck resource
A flexed budget
A non-binding constraint

10.18 H Co is preparing the budgets for the forthcoming period.

In January it has sales demand of 5,546 units of finished product. Production has a wastage level of 6%. Inventories of finished goods are constant each month.

Each unit of finished product requires 2 litres of raw materials, at a cost of $1.50 per litre. Inventory levels of raw materials are planned to increase by 500 litres each month

The materials purchases budget, in $, in relation to January's sales is:

$ [   ]

11 Budgeting for performance evaluation and control

11.1 Cranberry manufactures a single product and has produced the following flexible budget.

Activity level (units)	10,000	12,000	15,000
	$	$	$
Direct materials	20,000	24,000	30,000
Direct labour	50,000	60,000	75,000
Production overhead	45,000	50,000	57,500
Admin overhead	15,000	15,000	15,000
Total	130,000	151,000	177,500

What would be the estimated total cost of producing 13,500 units?

☐ $163,250

☐ $175,500

☐ $166,750

☐ $141,750

11.2 **What is a budget cost allowance?**

☐ A budget of expenditure applicable to a particular function

☐ A budget allowance which is set without permitting the ultimate budget manager the opportunity to participate in setting the budget

☐ The budgeted cost expected for the actual level of activity achieved during the period

☐ A fixed budget allowance for expenditure which is expected every period regardless of the level of activity

---

11.3 The production budgets for quarters 1 and 2 for a manufacturing company are as follows:

	Quarter 1	Quarter 2
Production (units)	5,000	7,000
	$	$
Direct materials	60,000	84,000
Production labour	52,000	65,000
Production overheads	70,000	70,000
Total production costs	182,000	219,000

If the budgeted production volume for quarter 3 is 8,000 units, what will the total production costs be?

$ ☐

11.4 A Co uses a variety of computer models in its budgetary planning and control process.

Three of these models are described below.

Which of these is/are a feedforward control model?

Select ALL that apply.

☐ Model 1: An exponential smoothing model is used to prepare a forecast of sales volumes each month. If these forecasts indicate that budgeted sales levels will not be achieved, the marketing department is required to take appropriate control action.

☐ Model 2: An inventory control model is used to determine minimum and maximum levels for each inventory item. The model produces an exception report whenever the actual inventory level reaches minimum level or maximum level, so that control action can be taken if necessary.

☐ Model 3: A target is set for month-end cash balances. A spreadsheet model is used to forecast the net cash flow and the resulting cash balance for each month. Control action is taken if necessary to achieve the desired cash balance.

11.5 The costs of the factory maintenance department for JEB appear to have a variable element dependent upon the number of units produced. The fixed element of the costs steps up when 10,000 or more units are produced. At an activity level of 12,000 units, the fixed element of the cost is $15,000. The variable cost per unit is constant.

Production volume	$
8,000	58,000
13,000	93,000

The cost at 11,000 units of production is:

$ _____

11.6 The following extract is taken from the production cost budget of L plc:

Output	2,000 units	3,500 units
Total cost	$12,000	$16,200

The budget cost allowance for an output of 4,000 units would be:

- ☐ $17,600
- ☐ $18,514
- ☐ $20,400
- ☐ $24,000

11.7 **A flexible budget is:**

- ☐ A budget which, by recognising different cost behaviour patterns, is designed to change as volume of activity changes
- ☐ A budget for a twelve month period which includes planned revenues, expenses, assets and liabilities
- ☐ A budget which is prepared for a rolling period which is reviewed monthly, and updated accordingly
- ☐ A budget for semi-variable overhead costs only

11.8 **Are the following statements about flexible budgets true or false?**

	True	False
Flexible budgets enable meaningful comparisons to be made between actual and expected revenues and costs.	☐	☐
In every variance reporting system which contains flexible budgets that compare budgeted and actual profit, there will be a sales volume variance.	☐	☐

11.9 Extracts from the flexible budgets of a manufacturing company are as follows.

Production and sales quantity	5,000 units	7,000 units
Budget cost allowance	$'000	$'000
Materials costs	50	70
Labour costs	65	77
Production overheads	80	84
Administration costs	35	35
Selling and distribution costs	15	19
Total cost allowance	245	285

What would be the total expenditure incurred in a period when 6,000 units are produced and 5,500 units are sold?

Administration costs are 100% fixed costs.

- ☐ $234,000
- ☐ $250,000
- ☐ $263,500
- ☐ $264,000

11.10 Which TWO of the following statements apply to feedforward control?

☐ It is the measurement of differences between planned outputs and actual outputs
☐ It is the measurement of differences between planned outputs and forecast outputs
☐ It is a proactive technique
☐ Variance analysis is an example

11.11 XYZ Co is preparing the production budget for the next period. The total costs of production are a semi-variable cost. The following cost information has been collected in connection with production:

Volume (units)   *Cost*
4,500 $29,000
6,500 $33,000

The estimated total production costs for a production volume of 5,750 units is nearest to:

☐ $29,200
☐ $30,000
☐ $31,500
☐ $32,500

11.12 **The original budgeted profit statement for a company, with all figures expressed as percentages of revenue, was as follows:**

	%
Revenue	100
Variable costs	30
Fixed costs	22
Profit	48

However, it has now been realised that the sales volume will only be 60% of that originally forecast.

The revised profit, expressed as a percentage of the revised revenue will be:
☐ 20%
☐ 33.3%
☐ 60%
☐ 80%

12 Standard costing and variance analysis

12.1 **Which of the following statements about standard costing is NOT true?**

☐ Standard costing is useful where products are non standard or are customised to a customer's specifications

☐ Standard costing provides useful information to assist management in controlling costs

☐ Standard costing makes it easier to value inventory

☐ Standard costing can be used to predict future costs and set budgets

12.2 **Which of the following could explain why a favourable labour efficiency variance has arisen?**

Select ALL that apply.

☐ Workforce motivated to perform well with higher bonuses for efficiency
☐ Hiring of more highly skilled workforce
☐ Over absorption of overheads
☐ Out of date machinery resulting in delays in the production process
☐ Higher quality material purchased

12.3 Capacity levels used in setting standard absorption rates for production overheads are often related to performance standards.

To which performance standard is budgeted capacity often associated?

☐ Attainable standard
☐ Basic standard
☐ Ideal standard
☐ Current standard

12.4 **Which of the following correctly describes a standard hour?**

☐ An hour during which no machine breakdowns occur
☐ An hour during which only standard units are made
☐ An hour for which standard labour rates are paid
☐ The quantity of work achievable at standard performance in an hour

---

12.5 Fowell O'Durr plc manufactures the industrial insect repellent Wingblitz. Standard data for budgeted monthly production of 1,000 litres is as follows:

	Litres	$
Chemical W	700	1,400
Chemical P	400	600
		2,000

Material inventories are valued at standard price, and inventories for the month of June were as follows:

	Chemical W Litres	Chemical P Litres
1 June	650	380
30 June	650	295

During June, 670 litres of Chemical W were purchased for $1,474 and 320 litres of Chemical P at a price of $1.60 per litre. 900 litres of repellent were produced in June.

What is the total direct materials price variance for June?

☐ $162 Adverse
☐ $180 Adverse
☐ $163 Adverse
☐ $166 Adverse

12.6 **Are the following statements about setting budget targets true or false?**

	True	False
Setting 'ideal standards' as targets for achievement should motivate employees to perform to the best of their ability.	☐	☐
Setting low standards as targets for achievement should motivate employees because they should usually achieve or exceed the target.	☐	☐

12.7 A company's annual sales budget includes 2,250 units of a product at a selling price of $400. Each unit has a budgeted sales to contribution ratio of 29%. Actual sales were 2,445 units at an average selling price of $390. The actual contribution to sales ratio was 27%.

The sales price variance to the nearest $1 is:

☐ $24,450 A
☐ $22,500 A
☐ $24,300 A
☐ $26,406 A

12.8 Cumberbatch Co operates a system of budgetary control involving the calculation of budget cost allowances.

The following figures are produced for the month of April.

	Budget	Actual
Production units	10,000	12,000
Labour costs: All variable	$8,000	$9,200
Contribution	$29,000	$32,900

What conclusions can be drawn from April's figures?

☐ There is a favourable variance on labour costs and contribution is higher than should have been expected.

☐ There is an adverse variance on labour costs, and contribution is higher than should have been expected.

☐ There is an adverse variance on labour costs and contribution is lower than should have been expected.

☐ There is a favourable variance on labour costs, and contribution is lower than should have been expected.

12.9 **Which of the following items should be included in the calculation of the sales volume profit variance?**

☐ Standard profit margin
☐ Actual profit margin
☐ Standard contribution margin
☐ Actual contribution margin

12.10 Budgeted fixed overheads for cost centre 1 during the last accounting period were $75,000 for apportioned overheads and $95,000 for allocated overheads.

A pre-determined machine hour rate is used to absorb fixed overheads into product costs.

Budgeted machine hours during the period were 1,800.

Actual fixed overheads were $177,770 and the fixed overhead volume variance was $6,500 favourable.

What was the fixed overhead total variance?

Fixed overhead total variance is $ ☐☐☐☐☐☐☐ Adverse/Favourable

12.11 **Which of the following is the least likely reason why standard costs might not easily be applied to road haulage and distribution services?**

☐ It is difficult to measure labour times reliably
☐ Variable costs are negligible
☐ It is difficult to identify a standard item for costing
☐ Standard costing applies to manufacturing industries only

12.12 A company's sales budget includes 1,200 units of a product at a selling price of $200. Each unit has a budgeted contribution to sales ratio of 31%. Actual sales were 1,080 units at an average selling price of $180. The actual contribution to sales ratio was 34%.

The sales volume contribution variance (to the nearest $1) is:

☐ $7,440 A
☐ $8,160 A
☐ $24,000 A
☐ $21,600 A

12.13 **Which TWO of the following would help to explain a favourable material price variance?**

☐ An increase in the quantity of material purchased helped buyers to earn unexpected bulk discounts.

☐ Improved processing methods meant that material purchases were lower than standard for the output achieved.

☐ The material purchased was of a lower quality than standard.

☐ A decision to reduce the raw materials inventory during the period led to a reduced level of material purchases.

12.14 **What is the name given to a standard which has remained unchanged over the years and is used to show trends?**

☐ Basic standard
☐ Current standard
☐ Attainable standard
☐ Ideal standard

12.15 Spendthrift Co purchased 6,850 kg of material at a total cost of $32,195. The material price variance was $1,370 adverse.

The standard price per kg was $ ⬚ **(to the nearest cent)**

12.16 During September, 300 labour hours were worked for a total cost of $4,800. The labour rate variance was $600 (A).

What was the standard cost per labour hour?

$ ⬚

12.17 A company revises its standards at the beginning of each year. Because of inflation, it sets its standard price for materials at the estimated price level for the middle of the year. During a control period early in the year, a fairly large favourable direct materials price variance was reported.

Which of the following would help to explain this variance?

1   The control period was early in the year.
2   Direct materials were purchased in greater bulk than usual.

☐ Both 1 and 2
☐ 2 only
☐ Neither 1 nor 2
☐ 1 only

12.18 The following variances are extracted from the monthly management accounts of SG Co.

Direct material total variance $800 (A)
Direct material usage variance $1,200 (F)

Which of the following statements is/are consistent with these variances?

1   High quality material was purchased, which led to a lower level of quality control rejects of completed output.

2   Rapid inflation affected the price of the company's raw material so efforts were made to reduce the quantity of material used per unit of output.

☐ 1 only
☐ 2 only
☐ Both 1 and 2
☐ Neither 1 nor 2

12.19 A company made 60,000 items in 80,000 hours. The budget was to make 57,000 items in 82,650 hours.

Will the fixed overhead capacity and efficiency variance be adverse or favourable?

☐
Capacity	Efficiency
Favourable	Adverse

☐
Capacity	Efficiency
Favourable	Favourable

☐
Capacity	Efficiency
Adverse	Adverse

☐
Capacity	Efficiency
Adverse	Favourable

12.20 A company has an adverse idle time variance of $6,000 and the standard labour rate per hour was $3 per hour.

If the actual hours worked were 12,000 hours, how many hours were paid for?

☐☐☐☐☐☐☐

12.21 **Are the following statements true or false?**

	True	False
(i) A favourable fixed overhead volume capacity variance occurs when actual hours of work are greater than budgeted hours of work	☐	☐
(ii) A labour force that produces 5,000 standard hours of work in 5,500 actual hours will give a favourable fixed overhead volume efficiency variance	☐	☐

12.22 A manufacturing company operates a standard absorption costing system. Last month 25,000 production hours were budgeted and the budgeted fixed production overhead cost was $125,000. Last month the actual hours worked were 24,000 and the standard hours for actual production were 27,000.

What was the fixed production overhead capacity variance for last month?

☐ $5,000 Adverse
☐ $5,000 Favourable
☐ $10,000 Adverse
☐ $10,000 Favourable

13 Further variance analysis

13.1 The following data relate to product Z and its raw material content for September:

Budget
Output   11,000 units of Z
Standard materials content   3 kg per unit at $4.00 per kg

Actual
Output   10,000 units of Z
Materials purchased and used   32,000 kg at $4.80

It has now been agreed that the standard price for the raw material purchased in September should have been $5 per kg.

The materials planning price variance for September was:

☐ $6,000 Adverse
☐ $30,000 Adverse
☐ $32,000 Adverse
☐ $33,000 Adverse

13.2   The following data relate to product Z and its raw material content for September:

Budget
Output   11,000 units of Z
Standard materials content   3 kg per unit at $4.00 per kg

Actual
Output   10,000 units of Z
Materials purchased and used   32,000 kg at $4.80

It has now been agreed that the standard price for the raw material purchased in September should have been $5 per kg.

The materials operational usage variance for September was:

☐ $8,000 Adverse
☐ $9,600 Adverse
☐ $9,600 Favourable
☐ $10,000 Adverse

13.3   The standard material cost of one unit of product F is as follows.

			$ per unit
Material G	9	litres × $4 per litre	36
Material H	6	litres × $2 per litre	12
	15		48

During March, 2,800 units of product F were produced, using 24,500 litres of material G and 20,500 litres of material H.

The materials mix variance is: $ [_____]   ☐   Adverse   ☐   Favourable

---

13.4   The standard material cost of one unit of product F is as follows.

			$ per unit
Material G	9	litres × $4 per litre	36
Material H	6	litres × $2 per litre	12
	15		48

During March, 2,800 units of product F were produced, using 24,500 litres of material G and 20,500 litres of material H.

The material yield variance is [_____]   ☐ Adverse   ☐   Favourable

---

13.5   Hardknott Co produces chemical NX57 by mixing two compounds. The standard material cost per unit of NX57 is as follows.

		$
Compound C1	5 litres at $110.40 per litre	552
Compound C2	7 litres at $45.00 per litre	315

During control period 13, the actual mix used was 1,098 litres of compound C1 and 1,350 litres of compound C2. Actual output was 200 units of NX57.

What was the total material yield variance reported in control period 13?

$ [_____]   ☐ Adverse   ☐Favourable

13.6 **Are the following statements about standard mix and yield variances true or false?**

	True	False
Mix and yield variances enable management to resolve problems with the quality of production output.	☐	☐
Persistent adverse mix variances may have an adverse effect on sales volume variances and direct labour efficiency variances.	☐	☐
Mix variances may be calculated whenever a standard product contains two or more direct materials.	☐	☐
When a favourable mix variance is achieved, there may be a counterbalancing adverse yield variance.	☐	☐

13.7 A company makes and sells three products. Budgeted and actual results for the period just ended were as follows:

Product	Budgeted sales units	Budgeted profit per unit $	Actual sales units	Actual profit per unit $
X	800	10	700	8
Y	1,000	6	1,200	6
Z	600	12	350	16
	2,400		2,250	

What was the sales mix variance?

☐ $1,475 (A)
☐ $1,475 (F)
☐ $1,800 (A)
☐ $1,800 (F)

13.8 **Are the following statements about sales mix and quantity variances true or false?**

	True	False
Sales mix and quantity variances are inappropriate for control report purposes when different managers have responsibility for sales of different products.	☐	☐
Sales mix variances can provide useful information for a company that wants to persuade customers to upgrade from a lower-cost and cheaper product to a higher quality and more expensive version.	☐	☐

13.9 **Complete the following using the statements below, to explain the importance of separating variances into their planning and operating components for the purposes of management control.**

Token (can use more than once):

ORIGINAL STANDARD
RELEVANT
REVISED
NOT CONTROLLABLE
CONTROLLABLE

Planning variances represent the difference between an ☐ , which is no longer considered to be a ☐ or accurate target, and a ☐ standard. Planning variances therefore represent differences between target and actual performance which are ☐ by operational management and so there is little to be gained from focusing management control action on such variances. An operating variance, on the other hand, represents the difference between a ☐ , realistic target and actual performance and as such are deemed ☐ by operational management. They therefore provide useful information for management control action.

13.10 SW plc manufactures a product known as the TRD100 by mixing two materials. The standard material cost per unit of the TRD100 is as follows:

			$
Material X	12 litres @	$2.50	30
Material Y	18 litres @	$3.00	54

In October 20X3, the actual mix used was 984 litres of X and 1,230 litres of Y. The actual output was 72 units of TRD100.

Calculate the total material mix variance for October 20X3.

The total material mix variance for October is:

$ ☐ Adverse ☐ Favourable

13.11 SW plc manufactures a product known as the TRD100 by mixing two materials. The standard material cost per unit of the TRD100 is as follows:

			$
Material X	12 litres @	$2.50	30
Material Y	18 litres @	$3.00	54

In October 20X3, the actual mix used was 984 litres of X and 1,230 litres of Y. The actual output was 72 units of TRD100.

Calculate the total material yield variance for October 20X3.

The total material yield variance for October is:

$ ☐ Adverse ☐ Favourable

13.12 A standard product uses 3 kilograms of direct material costing $4 per kg. During the most recent month, 120 units of the product were manufactured. These required 410 kilograms of material costing $4.50 per kg. It is decided in retrospect that the standard usage quantity of the material should have been 3.5 kg, not 3 kg.

What is the materials operational usage variance, if it is chosen to use planning and operational variances for reporting performance?

☐ $270 (A)
☐ $240 (A)
☐ $40 (F)
☐ $40 (A)

13.13 Two grades of labour work together in teams to produce product W. The standard labour cost of product W is shown below.

Labour grade		$ per unit
1	3 hours × $8	24
2	5 hours × $6	30
		54

During February, 800 units of product W were produced using 2,550 hours of grade 1 labour and 4,090 hours of grade 2 labour.

What labour mix variance arose in February?

☐ $60 (A)
☐ $60 (F)
☐ $120 (A)
☐ $nil

13.14 Two grades of labour work together in teams to produce product W. The standard labour cost of product W is shown below.

Labour grade		$ per unit
1	3 hours × $8	24
2	5 hours × $6	30
		54

During February, 800 units of product W were produced using 2,550 hours of grade 1 labour and 4,090 hours of grade 2 labour.

What is the labour yield variance which arose in February?

☐ $202.50 (A)

☐ $1,620 (A)

☐ $1,620 (F)

☐ $1,740 (A)

13.15 **In which of the following circumstances should the operational manager of a budget centre, rather than the purchasing managers, be held accountable for material price variances?**

1   When the operational centre uses excessive quantities of materials.

2   When the operational manager buys materials directly from suppliers.

3   When materials are purchased at short notice, at the urgent request of the operational manager.

☐   Circumstances 1 and 2 only

☐   Circumstances 1 and 3 only

☐   Circumstances 2 and 3 only

☐   Circumstances 1, 2 and 3

13.16 **For which of the following variances should a production manager usually be held responsible?**

☐   Material price planning variance

☐   Material price operational variance

☐   Material usage planning variance

☐   Material usage operational variance

13.17 A company sells two products X and Y. Product X sells for $30 per unit and achieves a standard contribution of $12 per unit, which is 40% of the selling price. Product Y, a new product, sells for $80 per unit and achieves a standard contribution of just $10 per unit, which is 12.5% of the selling price. Budgeted sales are 5,000 units of X and 3,000 units of Y.

However the sudden cancellation of an advertising campaign for Product Y has meant that sales for the product will be well below budget, and there has been some price discounting in an attempt to obtain sales for the product.

Which of the following sales variances, if calculated, would you expect to show a favourable variance for the period?

☐   Sales mix variance

☐   Sales price variance

☐   Sales quantity variance

☐   Sales volume variance

13.18 RB makes product ABC which contains three ingredients. The standard costs of the product is as follows:

	Budget	Actual
Direct material usage:		
Ingredient A	50 kg per unit	44,000 kg
Ingredient B	30 kg per unit	31,000 kg
Ingredient C	20 kg per unit	20,000 kg
Production units	10,000	9,000

Which two sets of data will need to be compared in order to calculate the materials mix variance?

☐
Ingredient A	44,000 kg at standard price
Ingredient B	31,000 kg at standard price
Ingredient C	20,000 kg at standard price

☐
Ingredient A	44,000 kg at actual price
Ingredient B	31,000 kg at actual price
Ingredient C	20,000 kg at actual price

☐
Ingredient A	47,500 kg at standard price
Ingredient B	28,500 kg at standard price
Ingredient C	19,000 kg at standard price

☐
Ingredient A	40,000 kg at standard price
Ingredient B	30,000 kg at standard price
Ingredient C	20,000 kg at standard price

13.19 The budgeted contribution for HMF Co for June was $290,000. The following variances occurred during the month.

	$	
Fixed overhead expenditure variance	6,475	Favourable
Total direct labour variance	11,323	Favourable
Total variable overhead variance	21,665	Adverse
Selling price variance	21,875	Favourable
Fixed overhead volume variance	12,500	Adverse
Sales volume variance	36,250	Adverse
Total direct materials variance	6,335	Adverse

What was the actual contribution for the month?

☐ $252,923
☐ $258,948
☐ $321,052
☐ $327,077

13.20 A company uses variance analysis to monitor the performance of a team of workers which assembles Product Q. Details of the budgeted and actual performance of the team for the last period were as follows:

	Budget	Actual
Output of Product Q	400 units	490 units
Wage rate	$25 per hour	$28 per hour
Labour hours	600 hours	720 hours

It has now been established that the standard wage rate should have been $27 per hour.

What is the labour rate planning variance?

☐ $1,200 (A)
☐ $1,470 (A)
☐ $1,200 (F)
☐ $1,470 (F)

13.21 The following budgeted and actual sales information relates to a budget period for a company that makes and sells three products.

Product	Budgeted sales Units	Budgeted profit per unit $	Actual sales
X	5,000	8	5,800
Y	3,000	14	2,700
Z	2,000	16	1,800

What was the sales quantity variance for the period?

☐ $1,000 (A)
☐ $3,240 (F)
☐ $3,800 (F)
☐ $8,550 (F)

13.22 A company uses a standard absorption costing system. The following figures are available for the last accounting period in which actual profit was $210,000.

	$
Sales volume profit variance	10,000 adverse
Sales price variance	7,500 favourable
Total variable cost variance	9,000 adverse
Fixed cost expenditure variance	5,000 favourable
Fixed cost volume variance	3,000 adverse

What was the standard profit for actual sales in the last accounting period?

$ [   ]

14 Modern business concepts

14.1   **Which THREE of the following are features of a just-in-time (JIT) purchasing and production system?**

☐   Maximum capacity utilisation.

☐   Pull scheduling: buying or producing at each stage of the supply chain only when the next stage in the chain wants the output.

☐   Kanban control: using a system of signalling work flow requirements using cards or other signalling devices.

☐   Greater visibility of what is going on, such as open plan work place layouts and coloured lights to indicate stoppages.

☐   Relying on a wide range of suppliers for raw materials and components, to ensure immediate availability of items.

14.2 **CIMA's definition of just-in-time (JIT) production is:**

☐ A system which is driven by demand for finished products, whereby each component on a production line is produced only when needed for the next stage

☐ A system in which material purchases are contracted so that the receipt and usage of material, to the maximum extent possible, coincide

☐ A system where the primary goal is to maximise throughput while simultaneously maintaining or decreasing inventory and operating costs

☐ A system that converts a production schedule into a listing of the materials and components required to meet that schedule, so that adequate inventory levels are maintained and items are available when needed

---

14.3 **Using the following list of quality cost classifications, place one of the options next to each one of the costs.**

Classification:

A   Internal failure costs
B   External failure costs
C   Appraisal costs
D   Prevention costs

Cost

Repairs under warranty	
Inspection of goods in	
Product design	
Lower selling price for sub quality goods	

14.4 Good quality saves money but the cost of quality can be analysed into cost of conformance and cost of non-conformance.

Which of the following costs is classed as a quality-related appraisal cost?

☐ Re-inspection cost
☐ Administration of customer complaints section
☐ Performance testing
☐ Training in quality control

14.5 **Which THREE of the following contribute to successful implementation of JIT?**

☐ Close relationship with suppliers
☐ Minimal set-up time and costs
☐ Non perishable raw materials
☐ Non perishable finished goods
☐ Similar production time across all stages of the production process

14.6 **Which THREE of the following are arguments against using variance analysis and standard costing in a TQM environment?**

☐ For standard costing to be useful for control purposes, it requires a reasonably stable environment.

☐ The ethos behind a system of standard costing is that performance is satisfactory if it meets predetermined standards.

☐ Cost is not important in a TQM environment.

☐ The control aspect of standard costing systems is achieved by making individual managers responsible for the variances relating to their part of the organisation's activities.

☐ Standard costs are set based on ideal standards rather than attainable ones.

14.7 **Which TWO of the following are features of World Class Manufacturing?**

☐ Dedicated cell production
☐ TQM
☐ Absorption costing
☐ Mass production

14.8 The following statements have been made about the application of standard costing systems:

Are the statements true or false?

	True	False
Standard costing systems are compatible with a Total Quality Management approach to operations.	☐	☐
Standard costing systems cannot be used in an industry that operates in a rapidly-changing environment.	☐	☐
Standard costing is well suited to organisations that produce items to customer specifications.	☐	☐

14.9 **Which THREE of the following are particular problems of JIT?**

☐ It is not always easy to predict patterns of demand.
☐ JIT is a demand led system.
☐ JIT makes the organisation far more vulnerable to disruptions in the supply chain.
☐ Wide geographical spread makes JIT difficult.
☐ There is a risk that inventory may become obsolete.

14.10 **A World Class Manufacturing manufacturer will have a clear manufacturing strategy aimed at which THREE of the following issues?**

☐ Meeting standard cost targets and avoiding variances
☐ Quality and reliability
☐ Flexibility
☐ Customer satisfaction
☐ Overhead recovery

14.11 **In a TQM environment, which THREE of the following are likely to be prevention costs?**

☐ Performance testing
☐ Cost of repairs under warranty
☐ Administration of quality control
☐ Training in quality control
☐ Maintenance of inspection equipment

14.12 Cakes N Co is a company which produces chocolate cakes. The following costs were incurred in April:

	$
Inspection of flour delivery received	200
Training cost for staff who melt the chocolate	1,000
Cost of taste tests after production	300
Oven breakdown repair cost	500

What is the total internal failure cost of quality for April?

$ [   ]

15 Environmental costing

15.1 **Which THREE of the following are ways of helping a business to become carbon neutral?**

☐ Encouraging more meetings between employees at different locations to discuss reducing carbon footprint

☐ Reducing energy consumption

☐ Increasing use of renewable electricity

☐ Offsetting

☐ Increasing use of electricity from national grid/country's central supply

15.2 **Which TWO of the following environmental costs would be classified as environmental external failure costs?**

☐ Inspection of product to ensure regulatory compliance
☐ Training of employees
☐ Cleaning up contaminated soil
☐ Government penalties and fines
☐ Recycling of waste products

15.3 **Are the following statements about environmental management accounting true or false?**

	True	False
A system of environmental management accounting provides environmental information for internal use by management, but not for external reporting.	☐	☐
Environmental management accounting systems typically make use of life cycle costing.	☐	☐

15.4 **According to one definition of environmental management accounting (EMA), EMA involves identifying, collecting, analysing and using monetary information about environment-related costs and savings, and also:**

☐ Investment returns on environmentally-friendly investment

☐ Physical information about the use and flows of energy, water and materials, including waste and emissions

☐ Impacts on the environment for which the organisation does not incur any direct cost

☐ The profitability of products, allowing for environmental costs

Which THREE of the following are advantages for a business of reducing greenhouse gases?

☐ Distinguishing the business from its competitors
☐ Driving down energy costs
☐ Keeping the office illuminated after hours will increase awareness of the company
☐ Improving corporate reputation
☐ Warmer office environment making staff happier to stay longer

15.6 Breadmagic Co is a company which produces loaves of bread. The following environmental costs were incurred in June:

	$
Forming environmental policy for Breadmagic	200
Training cost for staff who shape the bread to avoid wastage	1,000
Cost of fines for carbon dioxide (CO_2) emissions	1,500
Monthly maintenance cost of ovens to ensure efficiency	300

What is the total environmental external failure cost for June?

$ ☐

15.7 CT Co uses activity based costing and manufactures three products called the MyWalk, MyRun and MySprint. The following information is available for 20X2:

	MyWalk	MyRun	MySprint
Budgeted production (units)	1,500	3,000	1,600
Units per batch	500	1,000	1,600
Number of environmental inspections per batch	3	8	7

The total cost for environmental inspections for 20X2 is expected to be $70,500.

What is the total environmental cost attributed to MyRun for 20X2 (to the nearest $)?

$ ☐

15.8 **Which TWO of the following statements concerning environmental costing are correct?**

☐ Environmental costing leads to more accurate pricing.
☐ Environmental overhead costs are easy to measure.
☐ Using an activity based system, environmental costs become cost drivers.
☐ Like quality costs, environmental costs should be expressed as a percentage of profit.

15.9 AB Co uses activity based costing and manufactures two products called the Leaf and Conker. The following information is available for quarter 1:

	Leaf	Conker	Total
Budgeted production (units)	20,000	30,000	50,000
Kg of hazardous waste per unit	2	4	160,000
Total pollution inspections (3 per 1,000 units produced)	60	90	150

The total cost for disposal of hazardous waste for quarter 1 is expected to be $40,000 and the total cost for pollution inspections is predicted to be $15,000.

What is the total environmental cost attributed to Leaf for quarter 1 (to the nearest $)?

$ ☐

15.10 Gym Co is seeking to more accurately understand the environmental costs associated with laundering the towels used by members. It has decided to start charging customers for the use of a second towel.

In which of the following categories could the use of environmental costing lead to cost savings?

Select ALL that apply.

☐   Water and electricity consumption
☐   Use of detergent
☐   Staff costs
☐   Replacement towels

Answers to
objective test questions

1a Absorption costing

1a.1 The correct answer is: $0.55.

Different newspapers require different labour hours and machine hours as they are not identical.

Using a labour hour rate is not appropriate as production is more machine intensive than labour intensive. A machine hour is therefore more appropriate.

Number of machine hours = $(60,000 \times 0.4) + (80,000 \times 0.5) + (90,000 \times 0.3)$ = 91,000

Absorption rate = ($24,570 + $25,730) ÷ 91,000 hours = $0.55 per machine hour.

Distribution costs have been excluded as these are a non-production cost.

1a.2 The correct answer is: Actual overheads incurred are lower than the amount absorbed.

Over-absorption occurs when the overhead absorbed is greater than the actual overhead amount incurred. In other words, the actual overheads incurred are lower than the amount absorbed.

1a.3 The correct answer is: (i) and (ii) are true and (iii) is false.

Statement (i) is correct because a constant unit absorption rate is used throughout the period.

Statement (ii) is correct because 'actual' overhead costs, based on actual overhead expenditure and actual activity for the period, cannot be determined until after the end of the period.

Statement (iii) is incorrect because under/over absorption of overheads is caused by the use of predetermined overhead absorption rates.

1a.4 The correct answer is: $30,000.

	$
Actual fixed production overheads	X
Absorbed fixed production overheads (4,500 × $8)	36,000
Over-absorbed fixed production overheads	6,000

Actual fixed production overheads   = $36,000 − $6,000
                                      = $30,000

1a.5 The correct answer is: 240,000 units.

The total fixed production overhead variance ($100,000 Adverse) is the difference between fixed overhead incurred and fixed overhead absorbed (the under or over-absorbed fixed overhead.)

$100,000 Adverse = $1,300,000 − ($ \left(\dfrac{1,000,000}{200,000} \right) $ * × actual level of production)

$* \dfrac{1,000,000}{200,000}$ = standard overhead absorption rate

$100,000 = 1,300,000 − (5 × \text{actual level of production})$

$\dfrac{1,300,000 - 100,000}{5}$ = actual production

$= \dfrac{1,200,000}{5} = 240,000 \text{ units}$

1a.6   The correct answer is: $10,000 over absorbed.

OAR for last year   = Budgeted overheads/Budgeted machine hours
                           = $660,000/44,000 hours
                           = $15 per hour
OAR per unit   = $15 per hour × 0.2 hours/unit = $3
Overheads absorbed   = 200,000 × $3
                           = $600,000
Actual overheads   = $590,000

∴ overheads were over absorbed by $590,000-$600,000

= $10,000 over absorption

1a.7   The correct answer is: $117,400.

Absorption costing:

OAR = Budgeted overhead / budgeted production = $130,000/25,000 = $5.2/unit

As inventory has increased, absorption costing will report a higher profit than marginal costing.

The difference in profit   = change in inventory volume × fixed production overhead rate per unit
                            = 2,000 × $5.2
                            = $10,400
Marginal profit   = $107,000 (W1)
∴ Absorption profit   = $107,000 + $10,400 = $117,400

Working 1:

	$'000
Total contribution (20,000 × $15)	300
Less fixed production overhead	(118)
Less fixed selling costs	(75)
MC profit	107

1a.8   The correct answer is: Absorbed overheads exceed actual overheads.

Absorbed overheads exceed budgeted overheads – could lead to under-absorbed overheads if actual overheads far exceeded both budgeted overheads and the overhead absorbed.

If actual overheads exceed absorbed overheads then we have under-absorption.

1a.9   The correct answer is: $20,700

Units sold = units produced + opening units – closing units = 5,000 + 400 – 900 = 4,500 units

4,500 units × $4.60 = $20,700

Or

	$	$
Sales (4,500 × $20)		90,000
Less cost of sales		
Opening inv (400 × $15.4)	6,160	
Purchases (5,000 × $15.4)	77,000	
Less closing inv (900 × $15.4)	(13,860)	(69,300)
Gross profit		20,700

1a.10   The correct answer is: $78,000 over absorbed.

In a standard absorption costing system, overheads are absorbed based on the standard content of actual output.

$$OAR = \frac{\text{Budgeted fixed overheads}}{\text{Budgeted level of activity}}$$

$$= \frac{\$540,000}{1,080,000}$$

$$= \$0.50 \text{ per labour hour}$$

Absorbed overheads = OAR × standard content of actual output

72,000 units × 18 hours = 1,296,000 standard hours

Absorbed overheads = $0.50 × 1,296,000 =	$648,000
Incurred overheads	$570,000
Therefore over absorption	$78,000

1a.11   The correct answer is: $286.76.

	$ per unit
Material	20.00
Labour	69.40
Production overhead (14 hours × $12.58)	176.12
Total production cost	265.52
General overhead (8% of $265.52)	21.24
Total cost	286.76

1b Activity based costing

1b.1   The correct answers are: Number of production units, number of machine hours, number of labour hours.

Number of set ups and number of quality inspections would be used in an ABC system as opposed to a traditional absorption costing system.

1b.2   The correct answer is: $31.42.

Overhead (a)	Total number of cost driver units (W1)	Cost driver rate (a) ÷ (b) = (c)	Overhead absorbed for unit X (W2)
$488,000	61,000 machine hours	$8	$288,000
$85,000	50 set-ups	$1,700	$17,000
$162,000	36 orders	$4,500	$72,000
			$377,000

Amount absorbed per unit = $377,000/12,000 = $31.42

Working

1   (12,000 × 3) + (25,000 × 1) = 61,000 machine hours
10 + 40 = 50 set-ups
16 + 20 = 36 orders

2      $8 × 12,000 × 3 = $288,000
$1,700 × 10 = $17,000
$4,500 × 16 = $72,000

1b.3   The correct answer is: (i) and (ii) are false and (iii) and (iv) are true.

ABC is an alternative to traditional volume-based costing models, where production overhead is absorbed on the basis of the volume of direct labour hours or machine hours worked. However, it is still a form of absorption costing because production overheads are absorbed in product costs. (The difference is the use of multiple OARs.)

ABC can be used for costing services as well as products and although it looks at the cost of activities, it is not a method for identifying relevant costs for short-term decision making. However, by identifying cost drivers it can help to influence long-term decision making.

1b.4   The correct answer is: $58,500.

Total contribution = $8,100,000 + $1,000,000 = $9,100,000.

Contribution per unit = $9,100,000/130,000 = $70.

Cost pool	Overhead ($)	Cost per cost driver
Order processing	250,000	$5 per order
Sales force salaries	400,000	$20 per hour
Research	350,000	$35 per hour

Customer X overhead = ($5 × 400) + ($20 × 300) + ($35 × 100) = $11,500

Customer X contribution = $70,000

Customer X profit = $70,000 − $11,500 = $58,500

1b.5   The correct answer is: i, iii and iv are true. ii is false.

i   Short-term variable overhead costs should be traced to products using volume-related cost drivers, such as machine hours or direct labour hours.

Correct. Short-term variable overhead costs vary with the volume of activity, and should be allocated to products accordingly.

ii   Long-term variable production overhead costs are driven partly by the complexity and diversity of production work, as well as by the volume of output.

This statement is not completely correct. Many overhead costs, traditionally regarded as fixed costs, vary in the long run with the volume of certain activities, although they do not vary immediately. The activities they vary with are principally related to the complexity and diversity of production, not to sheer volume of output. For example, set-up costs vary in the long run with the number of production runs scheduled, not the number of units produced.

iii   Transactions undertaken by support department personnel are the appropriate cost drivers for long-term variable overhead costs.

Correct. For example, the number of credit investigations undertaken within the credit review department of a bank would be the cost driver of the department's costs.

iv   Overheads should be charged to products on the basis of their usage of an activity. A product's usage of an activity is measured by the number of the activity's cost driver it generates.

Correct. A mortgage might require three credit investigations and hence the mortgage should bear a proportion of the departments' costs to reflect the three credit investigations.

1b.6   The correct answer is: $112.91.

Rate per cost driver

Machining	$35,750/12,500 machine hours	= $2.86 per machine hour
Set-up costs	$5,250/10 production runs	= $525 per run
Materials handling	$17,500/40 materials deliveries	= $437.50 per delivery
Quality check costs	$22,500/15 checks	= $1,500 per check

Product Y overhead costs		$
Machining	2,000 machine hours × $2.86	5,720.00
Set-up costs	2 prod runs × $525	1,050.00
Materials handling	19 deliveries × $437.50	8,312.50
Quality check costs	5 checks × $1,500	7,500.00
		22,582.50

Overhead cost per unit = $22,582.50/200 units = $112.91

If you answered $2.86, this is the rate per machine hour.

If you answered $525, this is the rate per set-up.

If you answered $150.55, this is product Y's overhead costs divided by product Z volume.

1b.7   The correct answer is: Both statements are true.

Remember that the over or under absorbed overhead is made up of the fixed overhead expenditure variance, the fixed overhead efficiency variance and the fixed overhead capacity variance.

1b.8   The correct answer is: $0.40

Machining costs = (3 × 100,000) / [(3 × 100,000) + (2 × 150,000)] × $30,000 = $15,000

Set up = (100,000 / 500) / [(100,000 / 500) + (150,000 / 500)] × $40,000 = $16,000

General admin = 100k / 250k × $10,000 = $4,000

Checking = 200 / 800 × $20,000 = $5,000

Total overhead for M = $40,000

Overhead per unit = $40,000 / 100,000 units = $0.40 per unit

1b.9   The correct answer is: $0.90

Cost per movement	= $75,000/30,000	= $2.50
Number of movements per batch		= 18
Cost of movements per batch	= $2.50 × 18	= $45
Cost of movements per chair	= $45/50	= $0.90

1b.10   The correct answers are:

- Allocate overheads to cost objects.
- Allocate overheads to primary and support activities.

Production and service cost centres are features of absorption costing not ABC.

In no costing system are overheads allocated to resources.

1b.11   The correct answer is: $0.15

Number of batches produced
L	200,000/200	1,000
D	200,000/100	2,000
S	100,000/50	2,000

Number of set-ups required
L	1,000 × 2	2,000
D	2,000 × 3	6,000
S	2,000 × 5	10,000
		= 18,000

Cost per set-up = $270,000/18,000 = $15

Machine set-up cost per batch of L = $15 × 2 = $30

Cost per unit of L = $30/200 = $0.15

$30: is the set-up cost per batch of L.

$15: is the cost per set-up.

$0.54: is found by dividing the total cost by the total production level of 500,000 units.

1b.12   The correct answer is: ABC identifies value added and non-value added activities.

The results of ABC must be interpreted by management before they can be used to identify which activities add value and which do not.

The other statements explain why ABC gives more accurate information than traditional absorption costing.

1b.13 The correct answer is: $0.54.

$$OAR = \frac{\text{Annual machine set-up costs}}{\text{Total number of set-ups}}$$

Total number of set-ups = number of batches × set-ups per batch

			Batches	Set-ups
Product A	$\frac{80,000}{100}$	=	800 × 3	2,400
Product B	$\frac{100,000}{50}$	=	2,000 × 4	8,000
Product C	$\frac{50,000}{25}$	=	2,000 × 6	12,000
				22,400

$$OAR = \frac{\$150,000}{22,400} = \$6.70 \text{ per set up}$$

Product B has 8,000 set-ups so total cost for Product B = $6.70 × 8,000 = $53,600

Cost per unit of B = $53,600 / 100,000 units = $0.54

1b.14 The correct answer is: $120.

$$OAR = \frac{\text{Material handling costs}}{\text{Number of batches}}$$

			Batches
X	$\frac{50,000}{250}$	=	200
Y	$\frac{25,000}{100}$	=	250
Z	$\frac{20,000}{400}$	=	50
			500

$$OAR = \frac{\$60,000}{500} = \$120 \text{ per batch}$$

1b.15 The correct answers are:

Purchase order processing costs	A
Product advertising costs	B
Factory rent and rates	C
Direct labour costs	D
Product redesign costs	B
Material handling costs	A

1b.16 The correct answer is: $47.

Production set up cost	= $134,400/7	= $19,200 per set up
Quality control costs	= $55,200/9	= $6,133.3 per inspection

Total overheads for Tickles:

Set ups	2 × $19,200	= $38,400
Inspections	6 × $6,133.3	= $36,800
		$75,200

Per unit:

$75,200/1,600 units = $47 per unit.

2 Marginal costing and throughput accounting

2.1   The correct answer is: absorption costing profits would be higher by $27,000

Difference between absorption costing profits and marginal costing profits = difference between opening and closing inventory levels × fixed overhead absorbed per unit

Closing inventory	= opening inventory + production − sales
	= 980 + 13,250 − 12,500
	= 1,730 units
∴ Difference in profits	= (1,730 − 980) × $36 = $27,000

Closing inventory is greater than opening inventory which means some fixed overhead has been carried forward to be charged against the next period's profit under absorption costing.

∴ Absorption costing profit is greater than marginal costing profit.

2.2   The correct answer is: $107 ('000)

MC profit

	$'000
Total contribution (20,000 × $15)	300
Less fixed production overhead	(118)
Less fixed selling costs	(75)
MC profit	107

2.3   The correct answers are:

- Work in progress is valued at material cost only.
- It does not attempt to maximise profit.

The other options are incorrect because:

- Work in progress is valued at material cost only
- Material cost is added to products during production
- Only material cost is treated as a variable cost.

2.4   The correct answer is: Machine 2.

Machine 2 is the bottleneck machine as it has the highest utilisation of all three machines at 154%.

Utilisation rates:

Machine 1 (440/400)	= 110%
Machine 2 (615/400)	= 154%
Machine 3 (205/400)	= 51%

Max time required on machine 1: (5 × 50) + (2 × 50) + (1.5 × 60) = 440 hours

Max time required on machine 2: (5 × 50) + (5.5 × 50) + (1.5 × 60) = 615 hours

Max time required on machine 3: (2.5 × 50) + (1 × 50) + (0.5 × 60) = 205 hours

2.5   The correct answer is: $75,000 lower.

Inventory reduction of 300 units

Budgeted overhead absorption $\frac{\$500,000}{2,000}$ = $250 per unit

Reduction in profit:

300 units × $250 per unit = $75,000

2.6 The correct answer is: $3,100.

First calculate the number of units of inventory left at the end of October.

Closing inventory units = Opening inventory units + units produced – units sold.

= 0 + 4,000 – 3,600

= 400

The value of inventory using marginal costing is:

	$
Direct material	20,000
Direct labour	6,300
Variable production overhead	4,700
	31,000

Cost per unit = $31,000/4,000 = $7.75

400 units cost 400 × $7.75 = $3,100

2.7 The correct answer is: Lower.

Marginal costing will report a lower profit.

2.8 The correct answer is: 3.41

Throughput contribution per unit of J = $40 – $10 = $30

Throughput contribution per bottleneck hour = $30/0.01 hours = $3,000

Factory costs per year (overheads + labour costs) = $2,920,000 + (50,000 × $12) = $3,520,000

Factory cost per bottleneck hour = $3,520,000/4,000 hours = $880

Throughput accounting ratio = $3,000/$880 = 3.41

2.9 The correct answer is: 12,500

Any difference between marginal and absorption costing profit is due to changes in inventory.

Absorption costing profit	$2,000
Marginal costing loss	$(3,000)
Difference	$5,000

Change in inventory = Difference in profit/fixed product cost per unit:

= $5,000/$2 = 2,500 units.

Marginal costing loss is lower than absorption costing profit therefore inventory has gone up – that is, production was greater than sales by 2,500 units.

Production = 10,000 units (sales) + 2,500 units = 12,500 units.

2.10 The correct answer is: Marginal costing.

This is because it focuses on incremental costs. Total absorption and activity based costing involve notional costs (such as depreciation) and fixed costs (such as rent), which are never relevant to a decision. Standard costing does not necessarily deal with actual cash flow and is so unlikely to produce useful decision-making information.

2.11 The correct answer is: $180,000 lower.

	Units
Opening inventory	1,800
Closing inventory	900
Decrease	

$$900 \times \left(\frac{\$400,000}{2,000} \right)$$

= $180,000 lower

2.12　The correct answer is:

L2 should be produced before L1.

The product with the highest TA ratio should be produced first.

2.13　The correct answer is:

Absorption costing profits will be higher and closing inventory valuations higher than those under marginal costing.

Closing inventory valuation under absorption costing will always be higher than under marginal costing because of the absorption of fixed overheads into closing inventory values.

The profit under absorption costing will be greater because the fixed overhead being carried forward in closing inventory is greater than the fixed overhead being written off in opening inventory.

2.14　The correct answer is: $415,000.

Total contribution from each unit of service of X, Y and Z = $40 + $70 + $25 = $135

If equal quantities of X, Y and Z are sold, total contribution required to cover fixed costs and result in $40,000 profit is $140,000 (= desired profit + fixed cost).

Therefore: $\dfrac{\text{Total contribution required}}{\text{Contribution per unit of X, Y, Z}} = \dfrac{\$140,000}{\$135} = 1,037$ units of each X, Y, and Z

Sales value of one unit of each service is $100 + $200 + $100 = $400

Sales value required = $400 × 1,037 = $414,800

2.15　The correct answer is: (ii) and (iii)

The mark up used for both is arbitrary to an extent as it does not take into account external factors, such as the level of competition or the market conditions. Often a firm will adjust the final selling price to reflect such conditions.

The price elasticity of demand looks at the responsiveness of demand to a change in the price. Combining the revised level of demand and selling price it is possible to evaluate the impact on total revenue.

2.16　The correct answer is: None of them

It is actually a mark-up which will give a higher percentage for the same product. For example a 33% mark-up is the same as a 25% margin, meaning the first statement is false.

Using full cost pricing will only ensure that a profit is generated if the predicted level of overheads and volume of activity is correct.

Marginal costing applies similar principles to relevant costing, because it is based on variable costs. The reason it is not a form of relevant costing is that adding a profit margin/mark-up is an accounting adjustment and not a relevant cost.

2.17　The correct answer is: $5,060 lower

If marginal costing is used to value inventory instead of absorption costing, the difference in profits will be equal to the change in inventory volume multiplied by the fixed production overhead absorption rate = 110 units × $46 = $5,060

Since closing inventory are higher than opening inventories, the marginal costing profit will be lower that the absorption costing profit (so $5,060 higher is incorrect). This is because the marginal costing profit does not 'benefit' from the increase in the amount of fixed production overhead taken to inventory (rather than to the statement of profit or loss).

If you selected $4,600 lower or higher, you based the difference on 100 units of opening inventory.

3 Limiting factor analysis

3.1 The correct answer is: B.

	X	Y	Z
	$ per unit	$ per unit	$ per unit
Selling price	75	95	96
Variable cost	34	41	45
Contribution	41	54	51
Kg of material used per unit	2	1	3
Contribution per kg	$20.50	$54	$17
Ranking	2	1	3

If you chose option A, you ranked according to unit contribution.

If you chose option C, you ranked according to selling price.

If you chose option D, you ranked according to usage of material.

3.2 The correct answer is: $2,240.

Limiting factor is raw material.

	M	N	P
Contribution per kg of limiting factor			
$4.50/($1.25 ÷ $0.50)	$1.80		
$4.80/($1.50 ÷ $0.50)		$1.60	
$2.95/($0.75 ÷ $0.50)			$1.97
Ranking	2	3	1

Usage of the 6,000 kg

	Kg
2,800 units of P (× ($0.75/$0.50))	4,200
720 units of M (× ($1.25/$0.50))	1,800
	6,000

Optimum production with additional 1,000 kg

	Kg
(1,000 – 720) units of M (× ($1.25/$0.50))	700
100 units of N (× ($1.50/$0.50))	300
	1,000

Contribution obtainable:

	$
280 units of M (× $4.50)	1,260
100 units of N (× $4.80)	480
	1,740

Plus the original purchase price (1,000 kg × $0.5) = $500

Total prepared to pay = **$2,240**

3.3 The correct answers are:

- Marginal costing is appropriate for short-term pricing decisions.
- Absorption costing when used for pricing decisions includes the 'total-cost' of the product.
- Marginal costing is more appropriate than absorption costing for use in one-off pricing decisions.

3.4 The correct answer is: (1,000 × E) + (2,400 × D) + (3,000 × F)

	D	E	F
Contribution per unit	54	72	35
Labour hrs per unit	1	1.5	0.5
Contribution per limiting factor	54/1 = 54	72/1.5 = 48	35/0.5 = 70
Ranking	2	3	1

	Demand	Make				
Product F	3,000	3,000	3,000 × 0.5	= 1,500	5,400 − 1,500	= 3,900
Product D	2,400	2,400	2,400 × 1	= 2,400	3,900 − 2,400	= 1,500
Product E	2,200	1,000*	1,000 × 1.5	= 1,500		

*This is a balancing figure. We only have 1,500 labour hours left to use. Product E uses 1.5 hours per unit. So only 1,500/1.5 = 1,000 units can be made.

3.5 The correct answer is: $160.71

Throughput contribution per unit = selling price per unit − material cost per unit

Throughput contribution per unit = $26 − $7.25 = $18.75

Throughput contribution per hour =

$18.72 × $\dfrac{60}{7}$ = $160.71

3.6 The correct answer is: Product X.

	W	X	Y	Z
	$	$	$	$
	per unit	per unit	per unit	per unit
Selling price	56	67	89	96
Material	22	31	38	46
Throughput contribution	34	36	51	50
Time on bottleneck resource	10	10	15	15
Product return per minute	$3.40	$3.60	$3.40	$3.33
Ranking	2	1	2	4

3.7 The correct answer is: X, W and Y.

Total labour hours required to meet sales budget: (10,000 + 6,250 + 15,000 + 10,000) = 41,250.

Direct labour hours are therefore a limiting factor on production.

Product	W	X	Y	Z
Contribution per unit	$3.5	$2.0	$1.8	$4.0
Direct labour hours per unit	0.5	0.25	0.3	0.8
Contribution per direct labour hour	$7	$8	$6	$5
Priority for manufacture and sales	2nd	1st	3rd	4th

So make and sell 25,000 units of X (6,250 hours), 20,000 units of W (10,000 hours) and 25,833.33 units of Y with the remaining 7,750 hours available.

3.8 The correct answer is: $2,000.

First calculate the number of units of inventory left at the end of October.

Closing inventory units = Opening inventory units + units produced − units sold.
= 0 + 4,000 − 3,600
= 400

Using throughput accounting we include the cost of the materials only:

400 × ($20,000/4,000) = $2,000

3.9   The correct answer is to produce 400 As.

	A	B	C
	$	$	$
Sales price per unit	20	23	25
Material cost per unit	3	2	4
Labour cost per unit	5	10	7.5
Contribution per unit	12	11	13.5
Labour hours per unit	1	2	1.5
Contribution per labour hour	12	5.5	9
Rank	1	3	2

As demand for each product is unlimited produce 400 As.

3.10   The correct answer is: D.

	Z1	Z2	Z3
	$	$	$
Selling price per unit	15	18	17.00
Variable costs per unit	7	11	12.70
Contribution per unit	8	7	4.30
Labour cost per unit	$2	$4	$1.80
Contribution per $1 of labour	$4	$1.75	$2.39
Rank order of production	1	3	2

If you chose option A, you ranked according to contribution per unit.

If you chose option B, you ranked according to variable cost per unit.

If you chose option C, you ranked according to labour cost per unit.

3.11   The correct answer is: Up to but not including $14.50.

The shadow price of a limiting resource is the amount above the normal variable costs that will be added to the total contribution if one extra unit of the scarce resource (here direct labour hours) is made available.

This means that the company would increase contribution by paying up to $10 + $4.50 = $14.50 per hour for additional labour time. However, it would not pay exactly $14.50, as this would leave it no better and no worse off than if it did not have the extra labour hour.

3.12   The correct answer is: $420,000

	K	P
	$	$
Selling price	160	98
Mat C	20	0
Mat D	20	20
Labour	60	40
Contribution	60	38
Labour hours	3	2
Contribution per hour	20	19
Rank	1	2

Optimal production plan:

We are not told that there is a maximum demand for either product, therefore assume the 21,000 hours are used to manufacture Ks @ $20 per hour = $420,000

3.13   The correct answer is: 1,000 As, 2,000 Bs and 500 Cs

	A	B	C
	$	$	$
Selling price	50	68	94
Material A	(20)	(30)	(40)
Material B	(5)	(8)	(10)
Labour	(10)	(5)	(15)
Contribution per unit	15	25	29
Kg of Mat A per unit	2	3	4
Contribution per kg A	7.5	8.33	7.25
Rank	2	1	3

Optimal production plan:

		kg
Available		10,000
Make max number of Bs	(2,000 × 3)	(6,000)
Make max number of As	(1,000 × 2)	(2,000)
		2,000
Use rest to make Cs @ 4 kg	2,000/4 = 500	(2,000)

3.14   The correct answer is: (i) and (ii) are true. (iii) is false

Statement (iii) is incorrect as the shadow price is the maximum **extra** amount paid for one additional unit.

---

4 Relevant costs

4.1   The correct answer is: Adapting now will produce savings of $130,000 more than adapting in one year.

Sale of machinery would produce additional income of:	$800,000 – $600,000	= $200,000
Removal of machinery would save:	$100,000 – $110,000	= $10,000
Leasing machinery would cost an additional:	$80,000 – $0	= $80,000

A – There will therefore be additional savings of $130,000 ($200,000 + $10,000 – $80,000 = $130,000) by adapting now.

B – If you chose adapting now will cost $130,000 more than in one year, you calculated the correct amount but you got your costs and savings muddled up.

C – If you chose adapting now will produce savings of $110,000 more than adapting in one year, you probably deducted the savings on the removal of machinery instead of adding them.

D – If you chose adapting now will cost $110,000 more than adapting in one year, you probably deducted the savings on the removal of machinery instead of adding them and got the direction of the cash flow the wrong way round.

4.2   The correct answer is: $400,000

Price = variable costs saved of $150,000 + contribution earned on other products of $250,000

= $400,000

4.3   The correct answer is: $376.

	$
Additional purchases (5 tonnes × $50)	250
Relevant cost of material M already held:	
higher of $126 and (3 × $35)	126
Relevant cost total	376

If you chose $250 you only took the additional purchases into account and ignored the 3 tonnes in inventory.

If you chose $355 then you costed the 3 tonnes at the realisable value. This is incorrect as the opportunity cost is the higher of the two benefits foregone and in this case more is lost by not being able to use it on the alternative job.

If you chose $400 then you costed all of the material at the replacement cost. This is incorrect as the material is not in regular use.

4.4 The correct answers are:

- Notional costs
- Sunk costs

Avoidable costs and opportunity costs are both relevant as they are incremental and change as a result of a decision.

Notional cost is a hypothetical accounting cost used to reflect the benefit from the use of something for which no actual cash expense is incurred. It is not therefore relevant. Sunk cost is a term used to describe a cost that has already been incurred or committed and which is therefore not relevant to subsequent decisions.

4.5 The correct answer is: Replacement cost.

The relevant cost is the replacement cost of the material because material X is used regularly by the company in its normal business and is available from inventory.

4.6 The correct answer is: $25,230.

420 of the units required are already in stock. There are two alternative uses for these units.

They can be sold to realise $420 \times \$30 = \$12,600$, or they can be used as a substitute for material V. The saving would be $750 \times \$25 = \$18,750$.

This is therefore the best alternative use for the stock of material S. The opportunity cost of using them is the saving foregone. The remaining units will have to be purchased.

The relevant cost is $\$18,750 + (90 \times \$72) = \$25,230$.

4.7 The correct answer is: Both statements are true.

These are fundamental statements about relevant costing.

4.8 The correct answer is: $13,600.

The market value is $2 \times \$8,000 = \$16,000$. The current resale value is $\$16,000 \times 85\% = \$13,600$. The opportunity cost is the next best alternative foregone and therefore the answer is $13,600.

4.9 The correct answer is: $9,000.

Material Y is at replacement cost of $11 as in regular use. Material X – the 300 kg in inventory is at realisable value and that leaves 200 kg to buy at replacement cost of $7. Material Z is in inventory and has no other use so would also be costed at realisable value. $(300 \times \$3) + (200 \times \$7) + (500 \times \$11) + (100 \times \$12) = \$9,000$

If you chose $6,000 then you used historic cost for Y but all other materials were correctly treated.

If you chose $7,600 you forgot about the 200 kg of X that was not in inventory but treated everything else correctly.

If you chose $9,300 you used replacement cost for Z, even though it would not be replaced.

4.10 The correct answer is: Net realisable value.

This will, of course, depend on the manner in which they are to be disposed. It might be scrap value less any disposal costs or, if they are sold for an alternative use once work has been carried out on them, the net realisable value will be selling price less the costs of the further work.

Replacement cost is incorrect because replacement cost is not an appropriate relevant cost as the units are no longer required.

Variable cost is incorrect because variable cost is only relevant in certain circumstances (if net realisable value is the same as variable cost).

Full cost is incorrect because full cost includes absorbed fixed overheads, which are not relevant.

4.11   The correct answer is: Book value of the old asset.

All of the other options affect cash flow and are therefore relevant costs.

4.12   The correct answer is: An opportunity cost of $750 and an incremental cost of $1,500.

The relevant cost is an opportunity cost of $750 and an incremental cost of $1,500. If the material is not used on this order 500 kg could be sold to generate 1.50 × 500 = $750.

The other 300 kg would be purchased at the current price of $5 giving a total of $1,500.

Although the original $2,000 paid for the 500 kg in inventory is a sunk cost in this situation there is an alternative use for it. There is not an incremental cost of $4,000 since some of the material required is in inventory.

---

5 Multi-product breakeven analysis

5.1   The correct answers are:

- Total fixed costs/contribution per unit;
- Contribution required to break even/contribution per unit.

Breakeven point is the activity level at which there is neither a profit nor a loss. Alternatively, it is the activity level at which total contribution equals fixed costs.

The contribution to sales ratio gives the proportion of contribution generated by each $ of sales.

Costs to sales ratio is not a recognised ratio.

5.2   The correct answer is: $250,000.

Profit must increase by $100,000 to make a profit of $250,000.

Contribution to sales ratio is (1,000 − 600)/1,000 ie 40%

Therefore sales value needed to make a contribution of $100,000 = $100,000/40% = $250,000

5.3   The correct answer is: $2,000,000

	Superior contract $	Standard contact $	Basic contract $
Calculate contribution per contract	550	500	230

Calculate contribution per mix = 0.20 × $550 + 0.30 × $500 + 0.50 × $230 = $375

Calculate breakeven point = $\dfrac{\text{Fixed costs}}{\text{Contribution per mix}} = \dfrac{\$1,200,000}{\$375} = 3,200$ mixes

Calculate breakeven in terms of number of contracts

3,200 × 0.20 = 640 units of Superior

3,200 × 0.30 = 960 units of Standard

3,200 × 0.50 = 1,600 units of Basic

Breakeven in terms of revenue

= 640 × $1,000 + 960 × $750 + 1,600 × $400 = $2,000,000

5.4   The correct answer is: Lower.

The existing contribution to sales (C/S) ratios for each product can be taken straight from the table.

	R	S	T	
	$	$	$	
Calculate contribution per contract	0.6	0.4	0.5	Average C/S ratio = 22,000/45,000 = 0.49
Revised mix				
Sales (W1)	9,000	22,500	13,500	45,000
Contribution (W2)	5,400	9,000	6,750	21,150
Average C/S ratio (W3)				0.47

Workings

1   The new sales revenue mix will affect the sales of each product. Thus for product R, the new sales figure will be 0.20 × $45,000 = $9,000 and so on for the other two products.

2   Contribution is worked out by taking the current contribution to sales ratio (C/S ratio) and applying this to the new sales figure for each product. Taking product R again, the current C/S ratio is 60%, so multiply the new sales figure by 60% which gives $5,400 and so on for all three products.

3   This is worked out as $(21,150/45,000).

This is a long-hand way of doing the calculation but easier to understand if you prefer working from first principles. The examiner just multiplies through the existing C/S ratios by the new ratios thus:

(0.6 × 0.2) + (0.4 × 0.5) + (0.5 × 0.3) = 0.47

5.5   The correct answer is: 47.6%

	Basic	Standard	Advanced	Total
Revenue per mix				
Selling price ($)	50	100	135	
Contracts sold	750	450	300	
Total ($)	37,500	45,000	40,500	123,000
Contribution per mix				
Contribution ($)	20	50	70	
Contracts sold	750	450	300	
Total	15,000	22,500	21,000	58,500

Average C/S ratio = 58,500/123,000 = 47.6%

5.6   The correct answer is: There are two breakeven points: $5.64 million and $6.36 million.

	$
Total cost at sales of $6.8 million	6,560,000
Deduct step increase in fixed costs	(400,000)
Total cost excluding step cost increase	6,160,000
Total cost at sales of $5.2 million	5,440,000
Therefore variable cost of sales of $1.6 million	720,000

Variable cost = 720,000/1,600,000 = 45% of sales. Contribution/sales ratio is 55%.

	$
Total cost at sales of $6.8 million	6,560,000
Variable cost (45%)	(3,060,000)
Fixed cost	3,500,000

Fixed costs are $3.5 million at the higher sales level and so $3.1 million at the lower sales level.

When fixed costs are $3.1 million, breakeven sales = $3.1 million/0.55 = $5.636 million.

When fixed costs are $3.5 million, breakeven sales = $3.5 million/0.55 = $6.363 million.

5.7 The correct answer is: $914

Product	A	B	C	Total
	$'000	$'000	$'000	$'000
Sales revenue	360	720	200	1,280
Variable costs	90	240	110	440
Contribution	270	480	90	840
Fixed costs	180	360	60	600

Contribution/sales ratio   = 840/1,280   = 0.65625

Breakeven point in sales revenue   = $600,000/0.65625   = $914,286

With CVP analysis for a company that sells several products, a fixed sales mix has to be assumed.

5.8 The correct answer is: $5.188 million.

Weighted average sales price per unit = $[(20 \times 2) + (18 \times 3) + (24 \times 5)]/(2 + 3 + 5) = \$21.40$

Weighted average variable cost per unit = $[(11 \times 2) + (12 \times 3) + (18 \times 5)]/(2 + 3 + 5) = \$14.80$

Therefore weighted average contribution per unit = $\$(21.40 - 14.80) = \$6.60$

Weighted average C/S ratio = 6.60/21.40 = 0.3084112

Sales required to achieve target contribution of $1.6 million = $1.6 million/0.3084112 = $5.188 million.

If you chose $4.724m. You did not weight the sales and variable costs and so came up with a simple average contribution of 21 (C/S ratio of 0.3387).

If you chose $5.011m then you correctly calculated the average contribution of $6.60 and the BE mixes as 242.42. You then multiplied this by the simple average of $20.67 (not the weighted average) to get to the BE revenue.

If you chose $3.891m you forgot to add the target profit figure on.

5.9 The correct answer is: $2,802

When sales revenue is $1.5 million, total contribution is 45% × $1.5 million = $675,000.

This leaves a further $625,000 of fixed costs to cover. To achieve breakeven, sales in excess of $1.5 million need to be $625,000/0.48 = $1.302 million.

Total sales to achieve breakeven = $1.5 million + $1.302 million = $2.802 million

5.10 The correct answer is: $42,300

Contribution per unit

A $22
B $19
C $17

Contribution per mix

($22 × 1) + ($19 × 1) + ($17 × 4) = $109

Required number of mixes

(Fixed costs + required profit)/contribution per mix   = $(55,100 + 43,000)/$109
     = 900 mixes

Required sales of A

900 × 1   = 900 units
900 × $47   = $42,300 revenue

5.11   The correct answer is: $125,000.

       Breakeven point in units   = Fixed costs/contribution per unit

                                    = $50,000 / ($25 \times 0.4)$

                                    = 5,000

       Breakeven sales revenue   = 5,000 \times 25

                                    = $125,000

       Alternatively, sales revenue at breakeven point   = Fixed costs / C/S ratio

                                    = $50,000 / 0.4

                                    = $125,000

5.12   The correct answer is: $2,312,500.

       Sales revenue to breakeven = Fixed costs/ C/S ratio

       Therefore $2m = $800,000/C/S ratio

       Therefore C/S ratio = $800,000/$2m = 0.4

       Total contribution for targeted profit = Fixed costs + required profit

       = $800,000 + $125,000

       = $925,000

       To convert this target contribution into sales revenue we use the C/S ratio.

       $925,000/0.4 = $2,312,500

5.13   The correct answer is: $7,143,000.

       At the breakeven point, sales revenue = fixed costs/C/S ratio.

       From the question, fixed costs = $25 per consulting hour × 100,000 hours. The C/S ratio is given and is 35%.

       So sales revenue = ($25 × 100,000)/0.35 = $7,142,857 which is closest to $7,143,000.

       If you chose $875,000 then you multiplied the fixed costs by the C/S ratio and didn't divide which was the correct treatment.

       If you chose $1,786,000 then you only took the 25,000 per quarter and did not multiply this by 4 to give annual overheads. You then correctly divided by 0.35. If you got $219,000 you made the same mistake but then compounded it by multiplying by 0.35.

5.14   The correct answers are:

       Point A   Break even point if services sold in the order K, L, N, M.
       Point B   Multi product breakeven point

       Point A: is the company's **breakeven point** on the **assumption that the services are sold in order of their C/S ratio**, all of the service with the highest C/S ratio (service K 0.56) being sold first, all of the service with the second highest C/S ratio (service L 0.38) second, then N (0.35) and then finally M, which actually has a negative C/S ratio. We base the ratio on gross contribution (ie before any fixed costs).

       Point B: is the **average breakeven point** for RDF Co on the **assumption that the services are sold in the ratio 1,000: 2,300: 1,450, 1,970** until the breakeven sales value is reached.

5.15   The correct answer is: $1,692.

$$\text{Average C/S ratio} = \frac{(3 \times 27\%) + (2 \times 56\%) + (5 \times 38\%)}{(3 + 2 + 5)} = 38.3\%$$

       At breakeven point, contribution = fixed costs

$$\therefore \frac{\$648,000}{\text{Breakeven sales revenue}} = 0.383$$

       $\therefore$ Breakeven sales revenue = $1,691,906

       Therefore the answer is $1,692.

5.16   The correct answer is: $620,000

Breakeven sales revenue = fixed costs/weighted average c/s ratio

Contribution Y: 61 – 42 = 19
Contribution Z: 95 – 63 = 32
Total contribution for mix = (19 × 4) + (32 × 2) = 140
Total sales = (61 × 4) + (95 × 2) = 434
C/S ratio = 140/434 = 0.3226

Breakeven revenue = $200,000/0.3226 = $619,963 or $620,000 rounded up

5.17   The correct answer is: The contribution earned by Product B grows more quickly than the contribution earned by product A as sales levels increase

70% of the selling price of product A contributes to fixed overheads and profits, but for product B it is 74%.

If both products were made in the same department then product B would have a lower break-even point than product A, however the fixed overheads in department making B could be much higher than in A meaning that this statement is not true.

Variable costs are four percentage points higher for product A compared to B, but this is not the same as being 4% higher.

5.18   The correct answer is: 47%

Contribution = $500,000 – 90,000 – 80,000 – 30,000 = 300,000
Per unit = $300,000/600,000 units = $0.50

Breakeven units = $160,000/$0.50 = 320,000 units

Margin of safety: (600,000 – 320,000)/600,000 = 47%

6 Short-term decision making

6.1   The correct answer is: $7,776.

	$
N revenue ($32.40 × (8,100 × 0.9))	236,196
Further processing costs (8,100 × $16.20)	(131,220)
Share of joint costs $210,600 × (8,100 / 17,550)	(97,200)
Profit	7,776

6.2   The correct answer is: $80,000

If component B is purchased the contribution earned will be $45,000 and the variable cost saved will be $35,000. So the maximum that HM Co would be willing to pay = $45,000 + $35,000 = $80,000

6.3   The correct answer is: If those units bought from the subcontractor have the lowest extra variable cost per unit of scarce resource saved.

For example, if machine hours are a scarce resource, a company should minimise the extra variable cost of subcontracting per machine hour saved.

6.4   The correct answer is: Costs used for decision making never include fixed costs.

It is not true to say that costs used for decision making never include fixed costs. Fixed costs that arise as a direct result of the decision are relevant costs. They would therefore be included in costs used for decision making and for costs used for profit reporting.

6.5 The correct answer is: Division W and Division X only

	W	X	Y
	$'000	$'000	$'000
Contribution	140	420	60
Fixed overheads*	70	70	70
Profit	70	350	-10

*Fixed overheads specific to divisions = ($525,000 × 40%) / 3 = $70,000 per division

6.6 The correct answer is: Variance analysis.

Feedforward control is based on comparing original targets or actual results with a forecast of future results.

6.7 The correct answers are:

- The sales value of the joint product at the separation point
- The final sales value of the joint product
- The further processing cost of the joint product

Incorrect answers:

- The value of the common process costs
- The method of apportioning the common costs between the joint products

These are not relevant because the common costs remain unaltered regardless of whether the joint products are processed further.

6.8 The correct answers are:

- The costs of further processing
- The quantity of losses expected from further processing and their sales value
- The sales value prior to further processing
- The sales value after further processing

When deciding whether or not to further process a joint product after the separation point we do not require information on the joint process. The information we require relates to further processing.

6.9 The correct answer is: $53,410.

	$	$
Sales (480,000 × 1.15 × 0.97)		535,440
Direct materials (140,000 × 1.15 × 0.98)	157,780	
Direct labour 110,000 + (110,000 × 0.15 × 1.50)	134,750	
Variable overheads (50,000 × 1.15)	57,500	
Fixed overheads	132,000	
Total costs		482,030
Profit		53,410

6.10 The correct answer is: $270.

	$
Cost of labour (10 hours × $12)	120
Contribution forgone (at $15)	150
Relevant cost total	270

6.11 The correct answers are:

	S	A	T
Make	4,000	0	3,000
Buy	0	4,000	1,000

	S	A	T
VC to make $	20	36	24
Cost to buy $	29	40	34
Incremental cost to buy $	9	4	10
Hours to make	3	2	4
Additional cost to buy per hour	3	2	2.5
Rank to make	1	3	2

Only 24,000 hours are available, therefore need to make best use of these.

Hours available		24,000
1	Make 4,000 S @ 3 hours	(12,000)
2	Make 3,000 T @ 4 hours	(12,000)
		0

The remaining 1,000 units of T and 4,000 units of A will have to be bought.

The organisation's budget calls for 36,000 hours of machine time, if all the components are to be produced in-house. Only 24,000 hours are available, and so there is a shortfall of 12,000 hours of machine time, which is therefore a limiting factor. The shortage can be overcome by subcontracting the equivalent of 12,000 machine hours' output to the subcontractor.

The assembly costs are not relevant costs because they are not affected by the decision. The decision rule is to minimise the extra variable costs of subcontracting per unit of scarce resource saved (that is, per machine hour saved).

6.12 The correct answer is: $170

X is used regularly, so relevant cost = current cost = $100

Y is not currently used, disposal cost saved = $30

Z is not currently used, refund lost = $100

Overall cost = $100 – $30 + $100 = $170.

6.13 The correct answers are:

- Loss of control. By outsourcing part of the production process the company is effectively handing over control of issues such as quality to a third party.

- Loss of competitive advantage. An outsourcing partner can make the same parts and components for other competitors meaning that if too much of the production process is outsourced then competitive advantage can be lost.

- Loss of in-house skill. Shutting down parts of the factory and handing it over to an outsource company is likely to lead to a reduction in staff. This can make the decision to outsource hard to reverse.

Additional note: The decision to outsource can enable an organisation to tap into specialist knowledge which it does not currently possess. In addition it is likely to free up production capacity and reduce the amount of capital required.

6.14 The correct answer is: No product should be discontinued.

Much of the fixed overhead apportioned to each product is actually general overhead and would exist even if production ceased. The profits for each product can be recalculated as follows deducting only costs which relate to the products:

	K $'000	L $'000	G $'000	Total $'000
Sales	600	400	300	1,300
Cost of production				
Materials	(200)	(100)	(85)	(385)
Labour	(95)	(20)	(80)	(195)
Variable overhead	(75)	(10)	(20)	(105)
Specific fixed overhead	(90)	(40)	(12)	(142)
Selling costs	(30)	(20)	(50)	(100)
Profit before general fixed overheads	110	210	53	373
General fixed overhead				(308)
Net profit				65
General overhead previously apportioned to each product @ 80% of material cost	(160)	(80)	(68)	(308)

Each product therefore generates a profit before general overheads. This means that ceasing production of any of the products would lead to a fall in profits.

6.15 The correct answer is: $69,522.

Top tips. Note that as a first step, we need to deduct the proceeds of $18,000 for by product Z from the joint production costs of $140,000. This will give us the net joint production costs of $122,000. These will be apportioned to products X and Y on the basis of the final sales value of these products. As a third step, after the apportionment on the basis of sales value, we add the further processing costs to arrive at the total production costs for X.

	$
Joint production costs for W, Y, Z	140,000
Less: Proceeds from by product Z:	
$6 × 3,000	(18,000)
Net joint costs to be apportioned	122,000

Sales revenue from X and Y:

	$
X (2,500 units × $50)	125,000
Y (3,500 units × $60)	210,000
	335,000

Apportioning net joint costs on the basis of sales revenue:

$$X: \left(\frac{\$125,000}{\$335,000} \times \$122,000 \right) + \$24,000 = \$69,522$$

Top tips. The question is only asking for the total cost of producing X. The cost of producing Y is worked out below but it would not be necessary in the exam.

$$Y: \left(\frac{\$210,000}{\$335,000} \times 122,000 \right) + \$46,000 = \$122,475$$

6.16   The correct answer is: $4,500

	$
900kg in inventory could be sold for $3.50 =	3,150
Remainder will be bought 300kg × $4.50	1,350
Relevant cost	4,500

6.17   The correct answer is: Component Y only

	X	Y	Z
	$	$	$
Subcontractor price	8	14	11
Variable cost	5	16	10
Difference	3	−2	1

Component Y is cheaper to buy from the supplier than to make.

6.18   The correct answers are:

- Incremental costs
- Differential costs
- Opportunity costs

7 Linear programming

7.1   The correct answer is: $3J + 2T \leq 3,300$.

Let Jackets = J and Trousers = T.

The total available is 4,000m. However, 700 m is required for the contract (200 × 3 + 50 × 2) and therefore the amount to be considered in the decision is reduced to 3,300. The correct answer is therefore $3J + 2T \leq 3,300$.

If you chose $3J + 2T \leq 4,000$ you did not deduct the amount required for the special contract. If you chose $3T + 2J \leq 4,700$ you added the amount required for the special contract on to the total requirement incorrectly instead of deducting it and you mixed up J and T.

If you chose $3T + 2J \leq 3,300$ you mixed up T and J in your resource requirements.

7.2   The correct answers are:

- The contribution that can be earned from one additional unit of scarce resource.
- The premium that should be paid for one additional unit of scarce resource.
- The premium that should be paid for additional resources where there is no slack of that resource.

The following are not correct because:

- A shadow price is not the minimum that should be paid for scarce resource as this would mean that the amount paid would always exceed contribution that could be earned from it.

- It is also not the total that should be paid. The shadow price needs to be added to the normal price per unit to determine the total that should be paid.

- The other options are all ways of defining a shadow price.

7.3   The correct answer is: There is slack material.

This can be calculated as:

500 × 3 + 200 × 7 + 100 × 2 = 3,100. This means there are 400 units of slack material.

There is no slack labour as 500 × 2 + 200 × 1 + 100 × 4 = 1,600. This is the total availability.

7.4 The correct answer is: C = 45T + 35S

Contribution per unit of T = $130 – $25 – $40 – $20 = $45

Contribution per unit of S = $145 – $30 – $50 – $30 = $35

If you chose C = 45S + 35T, you got T and S the wrong way round. If you chose C = 35T + 30S, you incorrectly included the fixed overhead cost. If you chose C = 30S + 35T you incorrectly included the fixed overhead cost and you mixed up T and S.

7.5 The correct order is:

Define the variables	1st
Plot a graph	3rd
Identify feasible area	4th
Plot iso-contribution line	5th
Formulate constraints and objective function	2nd
Determine optimal solution	6th

7.6 The correct answers are:

- Identify the feasible area
- Formulate the constraints

Aside from these, linear programming requires a graph to be plotted, with an iso contribution line and the constraints and objective function formulated.

Allocating costs to cost pools and identifying cost drivers relate to Activity Based Costing (ABC), whilst identifying the breakeven point is a step in Cost Volume Profit (CVP) analysis.

7.7 The correct answer is: $2J + 1.5T \leq 2,325$.

Let Jackets = J and Trousers = T.

The total available is 2,800 m. However, 475 m is required for the contract ($200 \times 2 + 50 \times 1.5$) and therefore the amount to be considered in the decision is reduced to 2,325. The correct answer is therefore $2J + 1.5T \leq 2,325$.

If you chose $2J + 1.5T \leq 2,800$ you did not deduct the amount required for the special contract. If you chose $2J + 1.5T \leq 3,275$ you added the amount required for the special contract on to the total requirement incorrectly instead of deducting it.

If you chose $1.5J + 2T \leq 2,325$ you mixed up T and J in your resource requirements.

7.8 The correct answer is: 2,250.

Workings

$4W + 2T = 12,500$ (1)

$3W + 4T = 15,000$ (2)

Multiply equation (1) by two so we can eliminate T:

$8W + 4T = 25,000$ (3)

Subtract equation (2) from equation (3)

$8W + 4T = 25,000$ less

$3W + 4T = 15,000$

$5W = 10,000$

$W = 2,000$

Substitute W = 2,000 into equation (1)

$4 \times 2,000 + 2T = 12,500$

$8,000 + 2T = 12,500$

$2T = 12,500 - 8,000$

$T = 2,250$

7.9   The correct answer is:

Slack occurs when the **maximum** availability of a resource is not used in the optimal solution. Surplus occurs when there is production excess of a **minimum** requirement. If there is no slack then the constraints are said to be **binding**.

7.10   The correct answer is: $C = 17K + 15A$.

The iso-contribution line will represent the contribution (selling price less variable costs) that each product makes. The K makes $17 per unit, and the A $15 per unit. If you arrived at the figures of $7 and $6 you were incorrectly taking account of fixed overheads to calculate profit, not contribution.

7.11   The correct answer is: $32.50.

The shadow price for material X is the contribution that can be generated per m.

This is the unit contribution of $65 divided by the number of metres (2) = $32.50

7.12   The correct answer is: 0

The resource is not scarce and as such there is no shadow price.

7.13   The correct answers are:

- Total amount of scarce resource is known with certainty.
- Fixed costs are unchanged by the decision.
- There is no interdependence of demand between product.
- Unit variable cost is constant.

All are assumptions apart from the statement that says we assume units of output are not divisible. We have to assume that units are divisible. This is necessary to calculate optimal solutions and shadow prices. We also assume that there is no interdependence between products.

7.14   The correct answer is: $1.5J + 0.75T \leq 1,662.5$.

Let Jackets = J and Trousers = T

The total available is 2,000 m. However, 337.5 m is required for the contract ($200 \times 1.5 + 50 \times 0.75$) and therefore the amount to be considered in the decision is reduced to 1,662.50. The correct answer is therefore $1.5J + 0.75T \leq 1,662.5$.

If you chose $1.5J + 0.75T \leq 2,000$ you did not deduct the amount required for the special contract. If you chose $1.5J + 0.75T \leq 2,337.5$ you added the amount required for the special contract on to the total requirement incorrectly instead of deducting it.

If you chose $0.75J + 1.5T \leq 1,662.5$ you mixed up T and J in your resource requirements.

7.15   The correct answer is: $N - H < 0$

This can be seen if we substitute in 10 healthy items and 9 non healthy. The directive here is being followed.

$9 - 10 = -1$. This is less than 0.

7.16 The correct answers are:

- X = 700
- Y = 400

| 1 | 6x + 4y | = 5,800 |
| 2 | 14x – 10y | = 5,800 |

Multiply (1) by 10 and (2) by 4

| 3 | 60x + 40y | = 58,000 |
| 4 | 56x – 40y | = 23,200 |

(3) + (4) = 116x = 81,200

X = 700

Substitute in (1):

6x + 4y	= 5,800
4,200 + 4y	= 5,800
4y	= 1,600
Y	= 400

8 Risk and uncertainty in decision making

8.1 The correct answer is: 1,000 burgers.

Maximin = maximise the minimum achievable profit. The minimum achievable profits are when the weather is bad. The maximum profit when the weather is bad is achieved when 1,000 burgers are purchased.

8.2 The correct answer is: 3,000 burgers.

Table of regrets

| | Number of burgers purchased | | | |
	1,000	2,000	3,000	4,000
Weather				
Bad	0	1,000	2,000	4,000
Average	4,000	1,000	0	1,000
Good	9,000	6,000	3,000	0
Maximum regret	**9,000**	**6,000**	**3,000**	**4,000**

The lowest of these four maximum regrets is 3,000 when 3,000 burgers are purchased.

8.3 The correct answer is: $28,100

If the product development phase is successful the expected value is:

$0.5 \times 150,000 + 0.4 \times 50,000 + 0.1 \times (\$120,000) = \$83,000$

Note that this takes into account the cost of product development.

There is a 70% chance of this.

If the development phase fails then there will be a loss of $100,000.

There is a 30% chance of this.

So the overall expected value is:

$0.7 \times 83,000 + 0.3 \times -100,000 = 28,100$

8.4 The correct answer is: $32 (in '000s).

The best outcome without perfect information is project A with an expected value of $490 (000).

The best out come with perfect information is

- Weak demand – project C, net cash flow of $450 (000)
- Average demand – project A, net cash flow of $500 (000)
- Good demand – project B, net cash flow of $640 (000)

The expected value of these outcomes is:

- Weak demand – project C, $450 × 0.4 = 180
- Average demand – project A, $500 × 0.3 = 150
- Good demand – project B, 640 × 0.3 = 192

This adds up to 180 + 150 + 192 = $522 (000)

This is higher than the best outcome without perfect information by $32 (000). This is calculated as $522 – $490 = $32.

8.5 The correct answer:

Ignore risk when making decisions between projects that deliver the same expected value.

A 'risk neutral' decision maker will be interested in risk to the extent that it affects the expected value calculation eg if there is a high risk of a poor outcome they would take this into account in decision making. So they do not ignore risk entirely. However, if faced with two decisions with the same expected value they will not take risk of high or low returns into account when making a decision. They would be neutral between the two decisions.

'Risk-averters' try to avoid risk, and 'risk-seekers' seek risk.

8.6 The correct answer is: 104,000 units.

If the probability of a dry summer is 0.4 and the probability of a wet summer is 0.6. Therefore the expected value for sales is calculated as 0.6 × 120,000 + 0.4 × 80,000 = 104,000.

8.7 The correct answer is: 0.51

A profit of $1,000 and a loss of $3,000 are less than or equal to a profit of $1,000 and so the overall probability of a profit of $1,000 or less is 0.3 + 0.21 = 0.51.

8.8 The correct answer is: 0.82

Demand (a) Units	Probability (b)	Revenue (a)×$45 $'000	Variable cost per unit (c) $	Probability (d)	Total variable costs (a)×(c) $'000	Contribution $'000	Joint probability (b)×(d)
100,000	0.45	4,500	20	0.40	2,000	2,500	0.18
100,000	0.45	4,500	18	0.60	1,800	2,700*	0.27
120,000	0.55	5,400	20	0.40	2,400	3,000*	0.22
120,000	0.55	5,400	18	0.60	2,160	3,240*	0.33
							1.00

* Contribution higher than current level of contribution of $90,000 × $(50 – 21) = $2,610,000

∴ Probability = 0.27 + 0.22 + 0.33 = 0.82

8.9   The correct answer is: 63%

The probability of monthly contribution > $13,500 = 0.08 + 0.2 + 0.07 + 0.175 + 0.105 = 0.63.

Selling price	Probability	Cost per unit	Probability	Combined probability	Monthly contribution*
$/unit		$			$
20	0.25	8	0.20	0.050	12,000
	0.25	10	0.50	0.125	10,000
	0.25	12	0.30	0.075	8,000
25	0.40	8	0.20	0.080	17,000
	0.40	10	0.50	0.200	15,000
	0.40	12	0.30	0.120	13,000
30	0.35	8	0.20	0.070	22,000
	0.35	10	0.50	0.175	20,000
	0.35	12	0.30	0.105	18,000
				1.000	

* (selling price – variable cost) × 1,000

8.10   The correct answer is: $2,100,000

Contribution = Selling price – variable cost

= $120 – $40

= $80

Total contribution = 40,000 members × $80 = $3,200,000

Profit = $3,200,000 – $1,100,000 = $2,100,000

8.11   The correct answer is: Choice 4.

EV of Choice 1 = $9,500

EV of Choice 2 = (0.3 × 14,000) + (0.3 × 10,000) + (0.4 × 5,000) = $9,200

EV of Choice 3 = (0.4 × 10,000) + (0.6 × 9,000) = $9,400

EV of Choice 4 = (0.7 × 8,000) + (0.3 × 14,000) = $9,800

8.12   The correct answer is: $70

The worst outcome under each decision is as follows

Selling price	$60	$70	$80	$90

Demand level

	$'000s	$'000s	$'000s	$'000s
Weak	20	35	20	10

Using the maximin criterion, the best of these outcomes is 35, and this is achieved by selecting $70 as the selling price.

8.13   The correct answer:

Maximum regret (best outcome – actual outcome) is as follows

Payoff table

			Units produced	
	Best outcome	200 units	210 units	220 units
Demand				
200 units	**12,000**	0	12,000 – 11,600 = 400	12,000 – 11,200 = 800
210 units	**12,600**	12,600 – 12,000 = 600	0	12,600 – 12,200 = 400
220 units	**13,200**	13,200 – 12,000 = 1,200	13,200 – 12,600 = 600	0

As a footnote – the best decision using the minimax regret rule is to produce 210 units which has the lowest maximum regret (600).

8.14 The correct answer is: $200

The regret matrix has already been drawn so it's just a case of reading off the maximum regrets for each selling price and picking the lowest one:

Selling price ($)	140	160	180	200
Maximum regret ($)	50,000	60,000	40,000	30,000

The lowest maximum regret is $30,000 at a selling price of $200.

8.15 The correct answer is: 'A decision tree can be used to identify the preferred decision choice using the minimax regret decision rule' is false. 'A decision tree is likely to present a simplified representation of reality' is true.

Decision trees are used primarily to show decision options and decision outcomes in order to identify the decision option with the most favourable expected value. They cannot easily be used to show minimax regret values.

Decision trees may omit some possible decision options, or may simplify the possible outcomes. For example, a decision tree may show possible outcomes as 'sales demand 10,000' and 'sales demand 3,000' whereas a variety of outcomes between these two figures for sales demand may be possible. The decision tree is therefore likely to be a simplification of reality.

8.16 The correct answer is: $12 million.

At point D the alternative outcomes are to continue or abandon.

The option to continue has an expected value of:

$(0.6 \times 40) + (0.4 \times 20) = \$32m$

Less costs (20m)

EV of option $12m

8.17 The correct answer is:

Assume that the worst outcome will always occur and will select the largest payoff under this assumption.

Assuming that they will regret not having chosen another alternative and will therefore minimise the possible loss under this assumption is a minimax regret strategy.

Assuming that the best payoff will always occur and selecting the option with the largest payoff is a maximax strategy.

8.18 The correct answer is: $220,500

The expected value for fixed costs is:

$0.40 \times 100,000 + 0.35 \times 120,000 + 0.25 \times \$150,000 = \$119,500$

The expected value for variable costs is:

$0.35 \times 80,000 + 0.45 \times 100,000 + 0.20 \times \$140,000 = \$101,000$

The total expected value of costs is $119,500 + $101,000 = $220,500.

8.19 The correct answer is: 21.19%

$\mu = 80$ kg

$\sigma = 5$ kg

$z = \dfrac{84 - 80}{5}$

= 0.8 standard deviations above the mean. Using the normal distribution tables, the proportion between the mean and 0.8 standard deviations above the mean = 0.2881

Therefore the percentage of items weighting at least 84 kg is 0.50 − 0.2881 = 0.2119 = 21.19%

8.20 The correct answer is: Project C

Projects A and C both have the lowest level of risk, meaning that they would be attractive to a risk averse investor. However, project C gives a higher level of return for the same amount of risk, meaning that it would be preferable.

8.21 The correct answer is: 100

Market conditions	Probability	Purchase 100	Purchase 200	Purchase 300	Purchase 400
Weak	15%	50	(100)	(200)	(250)
Average	25%	120	120	250	100
Strong	50%	90	200	300	400
Exceptional	10%	80	300	400	500
Minimum return		50	(100)	(200)	(250)

Therefore choose to purchase 100 as this has the best, minimum return.

8.22 The correct answer is: 400

Market conditions	Probability	Purchase 100	Purchase 200	Purchase 300	Purchase 400
Weak	15%	50	(100)	(200)	(250)
Average	25%	120	120	250	100
Strong	50%	90	200	300	400
Exceptional	10%	80	300	400	500
Maximum return		120	300	400	500

Therefore choose to purchase 400 as this has the highest possible return.

8.23 The correct answer is: 15

Demand	Make 5	Make 10	Make 15	Make 20
Poor	-	30	25	40
Average	20	10	5	-
Strong	30	10	5	-
Max regret	30	30	25	40

Therefore choose to make 15 as this where the level of regret is lowest.

8.24 The correct answer is: $142,500

Selling price $	Variable cost per unit $	Contribution per unit $	Total contribution $	Probability	EV $
70	60	10	100,000	0.35	35,000
70	55	15	150,000	0.45	67,500
70	50	20	200,000	0.20	40,000
Total contribution					142,500

Note: Fixed costs have been ignored as these are not relevant when calculating contribution.

8.25 The correct answer is: $3.2m

EV @ A: $(0.7 \times 8) + (0.3 \times -3) = 4.7m$

Less costs of developing (1.5m) = $3.2m, as this is higher than the $2m for selling, the best option is to develop product G.

8.26   The correct answer is: $6m

		$m
EV with perfect information	$(0.3 \times 40) + (0.5 \times 30) + (0.2 \times 30)$	33
EV without perfect information		27
Value of perfect information		6

Need to work out the highest possible EV without perfect information:

Investment 1 = $20m

Investment 2 = $(0.3 \times 40) + (0.5 \times 30)$ = $27m

Investment 3 = $(0.3 \times 5) + (0.5 \times 25) + (0.2 \times 30)$ = $20m

8.27   The correct answer is: 175

		Daily supply of sandwiches (units)			
		125	150	175	200
Daily demand	125	$0	$11	$41	$60
for sandwiches	150	$18	$0	$22	$39
(units)	175	$41	$20	$0	$17
	200	$71	$45	$26	$0
Max regret		71	45	41	60

Therefore choose to supply 175 sandwiches per day as the maximum regret is lowest.

8.28   The correct answer is: 8.08%

μ = 50 cm

σ = 5 cm

$z = \dfrac{57 - 50}{5}$

= 1.4 standard deviations above the mean. Using the normal distribution tables, the proportion between the mean and 1.4 standard deviations above the mean = 0.4192

Therefore the percentage of tubes at least 57 cm long is 0.50 − 0.4192 = 0.0808 = 8.08%

9 Forecasting techniques

9.1   The correct answer is: A peak in the first three years of every decade, with a corresponding trough in the last five years of every decade.

Regular cycles involving an increase in the first half of each year, followed by a corresponding decrease in the second half of the year is an example of seasonal variations, which are short-term fluctuations in recorded values.

An increase of the same amount each year is an increasing trend.

A peak in the first three years of every decade with a corresponding trough in the last five years of the decade is an example of a cyclical variation, which is a medium term change in results caused by circumstances which repeat in cycles.

Occasional peaks which occur unpredictably but on average once every five years is an example of random variations, which are unpredictable.

9.2   The correct answer is: $12,120

Direct material cost per 1% activity = $40

Direct labour cost per 1% activity is not a constant amount at both activity levels, so this must be a semi-variable cost. Since production overhead is also a semi-variable cost the two costs can be analysed together, to save time (since the question asks only for a total cost in the answer).

	$
Direct labour and production overhead	
At 80% activity	8,200
At 90% activity	8,700
Change 10%	500

Variable cost per 1% change in activity = $\dfrac{\$500}{10\%}$ = $50

Substituting in 80% activity:

	$
Variable cost = 80 × $50	4,000
Total cost	8,200
∴ Fixed cost	4,200

Flexed budget cost at 88% level of activity

		$
Direct material (88 × $40)		3,520
Direct labour and production overhead:	Variable (88 × $50)	4,400
Fixed		4,200
		12,120

9.3   The correct answers are:

- a is a constant, a fixed amount;
- x is the independent variable, whose value helps to determine the corresponding value of y;
- y is the dependent variable, depending for its value on the value of x

9.4   The correct answer is: 326 units.

The trend must be 'moved on' from quarter 8 to 11, ie

330.625 + (3 × 6) = 348.625, and to this must be added the average seasonal variation of −22.5 ie 348.625 − 22.5 = 326.125 units.

9.5   The correct answer is: 675 units.

Forecast sales before seasonal adjustment = (53 × 17) − 258 = 643

Forecast sales after seasonal adjustment = 643 × 105% = 675 units

9.6   The correct answer is: 300,750 units

The forecast for sales units for the third quarter of year 7 is 300,750

Assuming that the first quarter of year one is time period reference number 1, the third quarter of year 7 is time reference X = (6 years × 4 quarters) + 3 quarters = 27

Therefore the trend Y = 25,000 + (6,500 × 27) = 200,500

Seasonally adjusted for the sales value of quarter 3

Y = 200,500 × 150% = 300,750 units

9.7 The correct answer is: $21,826

High activity	2,400	23,170
Low activity	1,650	20,770
	750	2,400

Variable cost per unit $= \dfrac{\$2,400}{750} = \$3.20$ per unit

Fixed cost (substituting in high activity) $= \$23,170 - (2,400 \times \$3.20)$
$= \$15,490$

Budget cost allowance for 1,980 units

	$
Variable cost (1,980 × $3.20)	6,336
Fixed cost	15,490
	21,826

Remember that you are dealing with **fixed** costs as well as variable costs. Do not make the mistake of dividing the total cost for production of 1,650 units by 1,650 to get a 'cost per unit' and then multiplying this cost by 1,980 to get the cost of 1,980 units. This would be a valid approach if you are dealing with variable costs only.

Similarly do not divide the total cost for production of 2,400 units by 2,400 to get a 'cost per unit' and then multiply this cost by 1,980 to get the cost of 1,980 units. Again this would be a valid approach if you are dealing with variable costs only.

You are dealing with a mix of **both** types of cost and you therefore first have to isolate the **variable** costs from the fixed costs.

9.8 The correct answer is: 315.63

Quarter	Sales	4 Quarter Moving Average	Centred Moving Average (Trend)
1	300		
2	320		
		293.75	
3	275		298.75
		303.75	
4	280		308.125
		312.50	
5	340		315.63
		318.75	
6	355		
7	300		

Therefore the trend figure for 1st quarter year 2 = 315.63

9.9 The correct answer is: An underlying long-term movement over time in the values of the data recorded.

A short-term fluctuation due to different circumstances which affect results at different points in time is a seasonal variation.

A medium-term change in results caused by circumstances which repeat in cycles is a cyclical variation.

A non-recurring fluctuation caused by unforeseen circumstances is a random variation.

9.10 The correct answer is: $1,739,000

The trend for year 8 quarter 4 is $1,632,000 and the trend is to increase by $25,000 per quarter.

The trend for year 10 quarter 1 is therefore $1,632,000 + (5 × $25,000) = $1,757,000.

The seasonal variation for quarter 1 is –$18,000 and so the sales forecast for year 10 quarter 1 is $1,757,000 – $18,000 = $1,739,000.

9.11 The correct answer is: At the mid-point of the period to which they apply.

A moving average is an average of the results of a fixed number of periods.

9.12 The correct answer is: $114,400

From the regression equation, variable cost per unit is $286. If production is 400 units, variable production cost is

$286 × 400 = $114,400.

9.13 The correct answer is: $17,600

			Difference
Output	2,000 units	3,500 units	1,500 units
Total cost	$12,000	$16,200	$4,200

Variable cost per unit = $\frac{\$4,200}{1,500}$ = $2.80

Fixed cost = 12,000 – (2,000 × $2.80) = $6,400

The budgeted cost allowance for 4,000 units = $6,400 + (4,000 × $2.80) = $17,600

9.14 The correct answer is: $3,990

$2,750/250 = $11 per unit including index, adjusting to the base year ($11/1.1) gives a base year cost of $10 per unit.

In month 3 the index is 114, therefore the unit cost is 10 × 1.14 =$11.40

For 350 units prediction: 350 × $11.40 = $3,990

9.15 The correct answer is: Prediction of future costs for activity levels within the company's relevant range
Regression analysis can be used to predict future costs, but only within the company's relevant range (ie the range for which it has experience of past costs) as extrapolation beyond this level could be unreliable. For example, beyond this range may result in extra fixed costs.

Using regression analysis does not identify the cause of costs or explain deviations from budgeted costs.

9.16 The correct answer is: $794,520

Month		Labour hours		Cost
January		15,000	$18,000 + (3 × 15,000) =	$63,000
February	(15,000 × 1.04)	15,600	$18,000 + (3 × 15,600) =	$64,800
March – December	(15,600 × 1.04)	16,224	10 × [$18,000 + (3 × 16,224)] =	$666,720
Total				$794,520

10 Budgeting for planning

10.1 The correct answer is: Budgetary planning

Strategic (or corporate) planning covers periods longer than one year. Operation planning is planning on a very short-term or day-to-day basis. Budgetary or tactical planning involves preparing detailed plans which generally cover one year.

10.2 The correct answers are:

- Purchasing budget
- Sales budget
- Marketing cost budget

All are functional budgets except for a cash budget. A functional budget is a budget of income and/or expenditure for a particular department or process. A cash budget does not relate to a function.

10.3 The correct answer is: $60,532

	$
40% of May sales for cash (40% × $55,000)	22,000
70% of April credit sales less 2% discount (70% × 60% × $70,000 × 98%)	28,812
27% of March credit sales (27% × 60% × $60,000)	9,720
	60,532

10.4 The correct answer is:

Zero-based budgeting is a method of budgeting whereby all activities are re-evaluated each time a budget is formatted.

'A method of budgeting that recognises the difference between the behaviour of fixed and variable costs with respect to changes in output and the budget is designed to change appropriately with such fluctuations' describes a flexible budget.

The other two answers are incorrect and do not describe any type of budget.

10.5 The correct answer is: Materials required for production – opening inventory of materials + closing inventory of materials

It may help you to think in terms of the inputs to a material purchases budget (opening inventory and purchases) and the outputs (closing inventory and the quantity used in production). The inputs should equal the outputs. Any one of the inputs or outputs can then be determined by manipulating opening inventory + purchases = closing inventory + used in production.

10.6 The correct answer is: The budgeted statement of cash flow, budgeted statement of profit or loss and the budgeted statement of financial position.

It does not necessarily contain all of the budgets prepared.

10.7 The correct answer is: All of the statements can be used to describe ABB.

ABB can be applied on a number of levels and hence various definitions are appropriate.

10.8 The correct answer is: There are no performance targets for managers.

The answer is that there are no performance targets for managers. There are usually performance targets in a budget, but with incremental budgeting these are often not challenging. There is no incentive with incremental budgeting for managers to reduce costs; on the contrary, there is an incentive for managers to make sure that they spend up to their budget limit in order to retain the spending in next year's budget.

10.9 The correct answer is: $86

	July $	August $	September $	October $
Sales	100	90	125	140
Opening inventory				
(Sales × 50%) / 125%	(40)	(36)	(50)	(56)
Required for this month's sales (Sales/125%)	80	72	100	
Closing inventory (see opening inventory in next month)	36	50	56	
Purchases	76	86	106	
Paid		76	86	106

10.10 The correct answers are:

A	Take action to adjust the capacity of resources to match the projected supply	4th
B	Determine the resources that are required to perform organisation activities	3rd
C	Estimate the production and sales volume by individual products and customers	1st
D	Estimate the demand for organisational activities	2nd

10.11 The correct answer is: Both statements are true.

By producing new plans at regular intervals, such as every three months, there may be a tendency for management to focus in changes to the plan rather than aspects of performance that should be controlled. They are time-consuming, and are only worthwhile when there is continual and substantial uncertainty about the future. (A simpler alternative if needed is to amend the annual budget when the budget is clearly unrealistic or out-of-date, by preparing an updated annual budget.)

10.12 The correct answer is: Management budgets may not be realistic in practice.

When senior managers impose budgets on managers below them in the organisation hierarchy, there is a risk that the imposed budgets will be unrealistic because senior managers may not have a full understanding of operational realities.

10.13 The correct answers are:

Difficulty in quantifying objectives

Difficulty in quantifying outputs

In private sector companies, objectives and outputs are fairly easy to identify, at least in the short term, as sales and profits. In the public sector, there are multiple non-financial objectives and many different ways of measuring output which creates complexity in the process. Budgeting within a spending limit should not necessarily make budgeting a difficult task.

10.14 The correct answer is: $109,200

	Month of credit			
		Sale		*Received*
	September	*October*	*November*	*December*
Factor × $100,000	15%	–	–	15,000
Factor × $120,000	–	20%	–	24,000
Factor × $130,000	–	–	60% × 90%	70,200
				109,200

10.15 The correct answer is: $660,000

		Hours
Labour hours required for production	(11,875 × 4)	47,500
Total time, including Idle time (5% of total hours required)	47,500/0.95	50,000

40,000 @ $12 = $480,000
10,000 @ $18 = $180,000
Total $660,000

10.16 The correct answer is: $15,615

		$
April	(0.2 × 18,000)	3,600
March	(0.5 × 17,000 × 0.99)	8,415
February	(0.15 × 16,000)	2,400
January	(0.1 × 12,000)	1,200
Total		15,615

Bad debts are ignored as they do not correspond to a cash inflow.

10.17 The correct answers are:

Does not affect the optimal solution in a linear programming solution – a non-binding constraint.

Is altered to reflect the actual level of activity – a flexed budget

Constrains what the business can achieve in the budget period – a bottleneck resource

10.18   The correct answer is: $18,450

		Litres
Litres required for sales	(5,546 × 2)	11,092
Total required for production	(11,092/0.94)	11,800
Plus increase in closing inventory		500
Required purchases		12,300

12,300 litres @ $1.50 each = $18,450

11 Budgeting for performance evaluation and control

11.1   The correct answer is: $163,250

Use the high low method to calculate the total fixed costs and the variable costs per unit.

	Units	$
Highest level of activity	15,000	177,500
Lowest level of activity	10,000	130,000
Difference	5,000	47,500

The variable costs = 47,500/5000 = $9.50

Substitute this value into one of the total cost equations to find the total fixed cost:

Total cost − (variable cost per unit × number of units) = fixed cost

177,500 − (9.50 × 15,000) = 35,000

Therefore total cost equation is: y = 35,000 + 9.5x

When x = 13,500, y = 35,000 + (9.5 × 13,500) = $163,250

11.2   The correct answer is: The budgeted cost expected for the actual level of activity achieved during the period.

A budget cost allowance is the expected expenditure in a budget which has been flexed to the actual level of activity. It includes a basic, unchanged allowance for fixed costs and an amount for variable costs according to the level of activity.

A budget of expenditure applicable to a particular function describes a functional budget and a budget set without permitting the ultimate budget manager the opportunity to participate in budget setting is an imposed or top-down budget. A budget cost allowance includes an amount for variable overhead and so a fixed budget for expenditure which is expected every period regardless of the level of activity is not correct.

11.3   The correct answer is: $237,500

Direct material costs = $60,000/5,000 × 8,000 = $96,000

Production labour (high-low method):

Units	Labour
	$
7,000	65,000
5,000	52,000
2,000	13,000

Variable cost per unit = $13,000/2,000 = $6.50

Fixed cost element:

$65,000 = FC + (7,000 × $6.5)

FC = $65,000 − $45,500 = $19,500

Labour cost in quarter 3 = $19,500 + (8,000 × $6.5) = $71,500

Production overheads are fixed at $70,000

Total cost = $96,000 + $71,500 + $70,000 = $237,500

11.4   The correct answers are: Model 1 and Model 3.

A feedforward control system involves forecasting future outcomes, and comparing these with desired outcomes. Control action is then taken to minimise or remove any differences. These two models are therefore feedforward control models. The inventory control model is a feedback control model, because it provides information on what has already happened, for comparison with a standard or plan (which in this case is the maximum or minimum inventory level).

11.5   The correct answer is: $81,000

The variable cost per unit = ($93,000 − $15,000)/13,000 = 6

Fixed element for activity up to 9,999 units = $58,000 − (8,000 × $6) = $10,000.

11,000 units = $15,000 + (11,000 × $6) = $81,000.

11.6   The correct answer is: $17,600

			Difference
Output	2,000 units	3,500 units	1,500 units
Total cost	$12,000	$16,200	$4,200

$$\text{Variable cost per unit} = \frac{\$4,200}{1,500} = \$2.80$$

Fixed cost = $12,000 − (2,000 × $2.80) = $6,400

The budgeted cost allowance for 4,000 units = $6,400 + (4,000 × $2.80) = $17,600

11.7   The correct answer is:

* a budget which, by recognising different cost behaviour patterns, is designed to change as volume of activity changes.

Flexible budgets are designed to flex with the level of activity.

A budget for a 12 month period is a fixed budget and used for planning. A rolling budget is updated but not in response to the level of activity, rather changes in the environment.

A flexible budget includes all cost types. Semi-variable costs have to be broken down but the flexed budget allowance will include total cost at that level of activity.

11.8   The correct answer is: Both statements are true.

Flexible budgets enable actual results to be compared with expected results for the same volume of activity, such as production and sales. To reconcile an original budgeted profit to actual profit with variances there must be a sales volume variance (measured in terms of either budgeted/standard contribution or profit, depending on the type of costing system used).

11.9   The correct answer is: $264,000

	Production costs	Selling costs
	$'000	$'000
Cost of 7,000 units	231	19
Cost of 5,000 units	195	15
Variable cost of 2,000 units	36	4
Variable cost per unit	$18	$2
	$'000	$'000
Total cost of 5,000 units	195	15
Variable cost of 5,000 units	90	10
Fixed costs	105	5

	$'000
Variable cost of selling 6,000 units (× $18)	108
Variable cost of selling 5,500 units (× $2)	11
Fixed costs (105 + 35 + 5)	145
Total budgeted cost allowance	264

11.10 The correct answers are:

- It is the measurement of differences between planned outputs and forecast outputs
- It is a proactive technique as it anticipates problems before they actually occur

Variance analysis is not an example of feedforward control because variance calculations are performed at the end of the period, which makes them an example of feedback control.

11.11 The correct answer is: $31,500

Use the high/low method:

	Volume	$
Highest activity level	6,500	33,000
Lowest activity level	4,500	29,000
	2,000	4,000

∴ Variable cost of 2,000 units is $4,000

∴ Variable cost per unit $\frac{\$4,200}{2,000}$ = $2

∴ Variable cost of 4,500 units = 4,500 × $2
= $9,000

∴ Fixed cost = total cost – variable cost (of 4,500)
= $(29,000 – 9,000)= $20,000

∴ Budget cost for 5,750 units = fixed cost + variable cost of 5,750 units
= $20,000 + (5,750 × $2)
= $31,500

11.12 The correct answer is: 33.3%

	Original	Revised
	$	$
Revenue	100	60
Variable costs	30	18
Fixed costs	22	22
Profit	48	20

The revised profit of $20 is 1/3 of the revised revenue of $60.

If you chose 20% then you calculated 20 as a percentage of the original revenue of $100 not the revised $60.

If you chose 60% you assumed that the profit would follow the pattern of the reduction in revenue. This is not the case.

12 Standard costing and variance analysis

12.1 The correct answer is: Standard costing is useful where products are non standard or are customised to a customer's specifications.

Standard costs work well when homogenous items are being produced, because the company can have an expected usage of inputs for each product, which can be used to value each item of inventory. This simplifies the bookkeeping as well as having the benefit of being useful as a future cost prediction tool. Variance analysis can be used to understand if the standard costs were achieved during a control period.

12.2 The correct answers are:

- Hiring of more highly skilled workforce.
- Higher quality material purchased.
- Workforce motivated to perform well with higher bonuses for efficiency.

The more highly skilled workforce is likely to operate more efficiently than the standard workforce, thus resulting in a favourable efficiency variance.

The purchase of higher quality material might result in less wastage of material and therefore less wastage of time in the production process which would give a favourable labour efficiency variance.

A workforce motivated to perform well with higher bonuses for efficiency will improve efficiency levels.

Out of date machinery resulting in delays in the production process would mean that labour would be less efficient, which would generate an adverse labour efficiency variance.

Over absorption of overheads does not explain a favourable variance for efficiency.

12.3   The correct answer is: Current standard.

- Budgeted capacity is associated with current standards.
- Budgeted capacity is not associated with basic standards.
- Practical capacity is associated with attainable standards.
- Full capacity is associated with ideal standards.

12.4   The correct answer is: The quantity of work achievable at standard performance in an hour.

For example if the standard time allowance per unit is 4 hours and 22 units are produced, output expressed in terms of standard hours will be 88 standard hours.

An hour during which only standard units are made is not correct. Many organisations make only standard units all the time. A standard hour is a measure of output based on standard levels of performance.

An hour during which no machine breakdowns occur is not correct. Hours free from breakdowns may be what an organisation aims for, but a standard hour is a measure of output based on standard levels of performance.

An hour for which standard labour rates are paid is not correct. This would result in a zero labour rate variance.

12.5   The correct answer is: $166 adverse.

The standard data can be used to determine the standard price per litre for each material:

W	=	$1,400 / 700 litres
	=	$2 per litre
P	=	$600 / 400 litres
	=	$1.50 per litre

The next problem is whether the calculation of the price variance should be based on materials used or materials purchased. Since stocks are valued at standard price, all of the price variance is eliminated immediately the stocks are received, so the variance should be based on purchases.

	Should cost	Did cost	Price variance
	$	$	$
670 litres of W ($\times$ $2)	1,340	1,474	134 (A)
320 litres of P ($\times$ $1.5)	480	512	32 (A)
	1,820	1,986	166 (A)

12.6   The correct answer is: Both statements are false.

There is likely to be a demotivating effect where an ideal standard of performance is set, because adverse efficiency variances will always be reported. It is important that adverse variances are not used to lay blame if targets have been set with the aim of motivation.

A low standard of efficiency is also demotivating, because there is no sense of achievement in attaining the required standards. Managers and employees will often outperform the standard or target when in fact they could have performed even better if they had been sufficiently motivated.

12.7   The correct answer is: $24,450 A.

	$
2,445 units (actual sales) should sell for @ $400	978,000
2,445 units did sell for @ $390	953,550
Variance	24,450 A

12.8 The correct answer is: There is a favourable variance on labour costs, and contribution is lower than should have been expected.

Actual cost of labour	=	$9,200
Expected cost of labour for a production level of 12,000 units	=	$8,000 × 12,000/10,000
	=	$9,600
Variance	=	$400 F
Expected contribution for a production level of 12,000 units	=	$29,000 × 12/10
	=	$34,800
Actual contribution	=	$32,900

Therefore, contribution is lower than should have been expected.

12.9 The correct answer is: Standard profit margin.

The sales volume profit variance is calculated as the difference between budgeted sales volume and actual sales volume, valued at the standard profit margin per unit. This approach is used when the company uses absorption costing. Under marginal costing the difference in units is valued at the standard contribution margin.

12.10 The correct answer is: $1,270 adverse.

Total variance	=	expenditure variance + volume variance
Expenditure variance	=	actual expenditure – budgeted expenditure
	=	$(177,770 – 170,000)
	=	$7,770 (A)
Total variance	=	$(7,770(A) + 6,500(F))
	=	$1,270(A)

12.11 The correct answer is: It is difficult to identify a standard item for costing.

With road haulage and distribution, drivers' times on the road are measured automatically. Variable costs can be high (labour and fuel for example). Standard costing is more common in manufacturing, but the principle can be applied to service industries.

The problem is to identify a standard item for which cost can be measured and variances subsequently calculated. In road haulage the standard would need to take into account distance travelled, size and weight and any special circumstances (eg refrigeration) which make it hard to establish a standard.

12.12 The correct answer is: $7,440 A

	Units
Budgeted sales (should sell)	1,200
Actual sales (did sell)	1,080
Difference	120
Valued at standard contribution	$7,440 A

Standard contribution per unit: 0.31 × $200 = $62

12.13 The correct answers are:

- An increase in the quantity of material purchased helped buyers to earn unexpected bulk discounts.
- The material purchased was of a lower quality than standard.

The unit price of material would be reduced as a result of the bulk discount and buying lower quality material.

The unit price of material would not be reduced by reducing the quantity purchased or improving the processing methods.

12.14 The correct answer is: Basic standard.

- An ideal standard is a standard which can be attained under perfect operating conditions.
- An attainable standard is a standard which can be achieved if production occurs efficiently. Some allowance is made for wastage and inefficiencies.
- A current standard is based on current working conditions.

12.15 The correct answer is: $4.50

Standard cost of material purchased – Actual cost of material purchased = Price variance

Standard cost = $32,195 – $1,370
= $30,825

Standard price per kg = $\dfrac{\$30,825}{6,850}$

= $4.50

12.16 The correct answer is: $14

	$
300 labour hours should have cost (× $c)	?
But did cost	4,800
	600 (A)

So 300 labour hours should have cost: $4,800 – $600 = $4,200

$4,200/300 = $14 per hour

12.17 The correct answer is: Both 1 and 2

Statement (1) is consistent with a favourable materials price variance. In a period of inflation, and with a **mid-year standard price**, reported variances early in the year would probably be favourable.

Statement (2) is consistent with a favourable materials price variance. Bulk purchase discounts may **reduce the unit price paid for materials.**

12.18 The correct answer is: Both 1 and 2

The direct material price variance is $2,000 adverse ($800 adverse – $1,200 favourable).

Both statements are consistent with the variances, because both situations would lead to a **higher price** for materials (adverse material price variance) and **lower usage** (favourable material usage variance).

12.19 The correct answer is:

Capacity	Efficiency
Adverse	Favourable

The standard time per unit was budgeted at 1.45 hours (82,650/57,000). Actual production should therefore have taken 60,000 × 1.45 = 87,000, but did take 80,000 hours meaning it was favourable.

The original plan was to work 82,650 units, but only 80,000 hours were worked, meaning that the factory operated below capacity.

12.20 The correct answer is: 14,000 hours

$6,000 variance @ $3 per hour = 2,000 labour hours.

Actual hours worked were 12,000 meaning that 14,000 hours must have been paid.

12.21 The correct answer is: (i) is true and (ii) is false.

Statement (i) is true. Statement (ii) is false. Producing 5,000 standard hours of work in 5,500 hours would give rise to an adverse fixed overhead volume efficiency variance.

12.22 The correct answer is $5,000 Adverse

Standard fixed overhead absorption rate per hour = $125,000/25,000 = $5 per hour

Fixed overhead volume capacity variance

Budgeted hours of work	25,000 hrs
Actual hours of work	24,000 hrs
Fixed overhead volume capacity variance	1,000 hrs (A)
x standard fixed overhead absorption rate per hour	× $5
Fixed overhead volume capacity variance in $	$5,000 (A)

13 Further variance analysis

13.1 The correct answer is: $30,000 adverse.

		$
Materials price planning variance		
Original standard cost of revised standard usage for actual output:		
($4.00 × 3 kg × 10,000)	=	120,000
Revised standard cost of revised standard usage for actual output		
($5.00 × 3 kg × 10,000)	=	150,000
		30,000 A

13.2 The correct answer is: $10,000 adverse.

Materials operational usage variance	kg
10,000 units should use 3 kg per unit	30,000
10,000 units did use	32,000
	2,000 A

2,000 kg at standard revised cost of $5 per kg = $10,000 adverse

13.3 The correct answer is: $5,000 favourable

Standard mix: $\frac{3}{5}$ G, $\frac{2}{5}$ H

Material	Actual input	Standard mix of actual input*	Variance	× standard price	Variance
	Litres	Litres	Litres	$	$
G	24,500	27,000	2,500 (F)	4	10,000 (F)
H	20,500	18,000	2,500 (A)	2	5,000 (A)
	45,000	45,000	–		5,000 (F)

*45,000 × (9/15) = 27,000 litres
45,000 × (6/15) = 18,000 litres

Alternative approach

Standard weighted average price of materials = $\frac{\$48}{15 \text{ litres}}$ = $3.20 per litre

Material	Actual input	Standard mix of actual input	Difference	× difference between weighted average price and standard price	Mix variance
	Litres	Litres	Litres	$	$
G	24,500	27,000	(2,500) less	($3.20 – $4) $0.80 more	2,000 (F)
H	20,500	18,000	2,500 more	($3.20 – $2) $1.20	3,000 (F)
	45,000	45,000	–		5,000 (F)

13.4 The correct answer is: 9,600 A.

Total input of 45,000 litres should have yielded (÷ 15 litres)	3,000 units
but did yield	2,800 units
Yield variance in units	200 units (A)
× standard material cost per unit of output	× $48
	$9,600 A

13.5 The correct answer is: $3,468 Adverse.

(1,098 + 1,350) litres should have yielded (÷12)	204 units
but did yield	200 units
Yield variance in units	4 (A) units
× standard cost per unit ($552 + 315)	× $867
	$3,468 (A)

13.6 The correct answer is: Statements 1, 2 and 4 are true.

Mix and yield variances measure costs and output quantities, not quality. A potential problem is that persistent favourable mix variances may have an adverse effect on sales volume variances and direct labour efficiency variances, because the cheaper materials mix may affect the quality of the product sold to customers and also make the product more difficult to handle. These consequences could lead to adverse sales volume and labour efficiency variances.

Mix variances can only be calculated when a product contains two or more materials that can be mixed together in different proportions. For example, calculating a mix variance for the production of a bicycle out of its component parts would be meaningless. It is important to be aware of the interdependence between variances: a favourable mix variance, meaning a cheaper mix of materials in a product, may result in adverse total output of the product (adverse yield).

However, it is not the case that a favourable mix variance will always result in an adverse yield variance.

13.7 The correct answer is: $1,475 (A).

Sales mix variance

	Actual sales Std mix (W1)	Actual qty Act mix	Difference in units		× std profit $	Variance $	
X	750	700	50	(A)	10	500	(A)
Y	937.5	1,200	262.5	(F)	6	1,575	(F)
Z	562.5	350	212.5	(A)	12	2,550	(A)
	2,250	2,250	–			1,475	(A)

Working

Actual sales at std mix:

X	2,250 × (800/2,400) =	750
Y	2,250 × (1,000/2,400) =	937.5
Z	2,250 × (600/2,400) =	562.5

13.8 The correct answer is: They are both true.

If the sales mix is not a controllable item, and managers do not have control over it, sales mix variances do not provide meaningful control information. Sales volume variances for individual products would be more appropriate. If a company is trying to encourage customers to shift from one product to another, sales mix variances could provide useful control information, although other measures of performance might be just as good and possibly more suitable.

13.9 The correct answer is:

Planning variances represent the difference between an **original standard**, which is no longer considered to be a **relevant** or accurate target, and a **revised** standard. Planning variances therefore represent differences between target and actual performance which are **not controllable** by operational management and so there is little to be gained from focusing management control action on such variances. An operating variance, on the other hand, represents the difference between a **revised**, realistic target and actual performance and as such are deemed **controllable** by operational management. They therefore provide useful information for management control action.

13.10 The correct answer is: $49.20 Favourable.

Product TRD100

	Standard mix Litres	Actual mix Litres	Difference Litres	Price $	Variance $	
X	885.6	984	98.4	2.50	246.0	(A)
Y	1,328.4	1,230	98.4	3.00	295.2	(F)
Total	2,214.0	2,214	nil		49.2	(F)

13.11 The correct answer is: $151.20 Adverse.

Expected output of product TRD100 $\dfrac{2{,}214}{30}$ =   73.8 units

Actual output	=	72.0 units
Shortfall	=	1.8 units
1.8 units × $84/unit	=	$151.20(A)

13.12 The correct answer is: 40 (F).

	Kg
120 units of product should use (× 3.5 kg)	420
They did use	410
Operational usage variance in kg	10 (F)

Operational usage variance in $ (× standard price per kg $4) = $40 (F)

13.13 The correct answer is: $120 (A)

Standard mix is $\frac{3}{8}$ grade 1, $\frac{5}{8}$ grade 2.

Labour grade	Actual input hours	Standard mix of actual input hours	Variance hours		× standard rate $	Variance $	
1	2,550	2,490	60	(A)	8	480	(A)
2	4,090	4,150	60	(F)	6	360	(F)
	6,640	6,640	–			120	(A)

Alternative approach

Labour grade	Actual input hours	Standard mix of actual input hours	Difference hours	× difference between weighted average rate and standard rate $		Mix variance $
1	2,550	2,490	60	($6.75* − $8)	(1.25)	75 (A)
2	4,090	4,150	(60)	($6.75 − $6)	0.75	45 (A)
	6,640	6,640				120 (A)

*$54/8

13.14 The correct answer is: $1,620 (A)

6,640 hours of labour should yield (÷ 8 hours)	830	Units
but did yield	800	Units
Yield variance in units	30	Units (A)
× standard labour cost per unit of output	× $54	
Yield variance in $	$1,620	(A)

If you selected $202.50 (A) you calculated the correct yield variance in units but you evaluated it at the average standard rate per labour hour ($6.75).

If you selected $1,620 (F) you calculated the variance correctly but misinterpreted it as favourable.

$1,740 (A) is the efficiency variance, which is the total of the variances for labour mix and yield.

13.15 The correct answer is: Circumstances 2 and 3 only.

Excessive usage of materials is reported as a usage variance, not a price variance. The operational manager should be responsible for price variances when they have responsibility for materials purchasing, or when the production department asks for an urgent materials order, resulting in higher purchasing prices than normal.

13.16 The correct answer is: Material usage operational variance

Material usage variances are in the production manager's control. Material price variances are usually the responsibility of the purchasing manager.

Operational variances can be controlled by a line manager. In this instance the production manager can control efficiencies within the production process, influencing the operational variance. Planning variances are attributable to the manager responsible for approving the original standard, usually a more senior director.

13.17 The correct answer is: Sales mix variance.

The loss of the advertising campaign means that sales of Product Y will be less than budgeted, which should lead us to expect adverse sales volume variance for Y and an adverse sales quantity variance for both products together. The price discounting for Product Y should lead us to expect an adverse sales price variance. The increase in the proportion of Product X units sold in the total sales mix should lead us to expect a favourable sales mix variance, because Product X has a bigger standard contribution, both per unit and per $1 of standard sales price, than Product Y.

13.18 The correct answer is:

Ingredient A	44,000 kg at standard price
Ingredient B	31,000 kg at standard price
Ingredient C	20,000 kg at standard price

Ingredient A	47,500 kg at standard price
Ingredient B	28,500 kg at standard price
Ingredient C	19,000 kg at standard price

The mix variance should always be based on standard price. It should compare the actual quantities in the actual mix to the actual quantities in the standard mix.

13.19 The correct answer is: $258,948

Standard marginal costing reconciliation

	$
Original budgeted contribution	290,000
Sales volume variance	(36,250)
Standard contribution from actual sales	253,750
Selling price variance	21,875
	275,625
Variable cost variances	
Total direct material variance	(6,335)
Total direct labour variance	11,323
Total variable overhead variance	(21,665)
Actual contribution	258,948

13.20 The correct answer is: $1,470 (A)

Standard hours per unit = 600/400 = 1.5

Original standard cost = 490 units × 1.5 × $25	$18,375
Revised standard cost = 490 units × 1.5 × $27	$19,845
Labour rate planning variance	$1,470 (A)

13.21 The correct answer is: $3,240 (F).

Total actual sales = 5,800 + 2,700 + 1,800 = $10,300

Actual sales in standard mix:

X	$10,300 × 5/10 =	$5,150
Y	$10,300 × 3/10 =	$3,090
Z	$10,300 × 2/10 =	$2,060
		$10,300

	Actual sales Std mix $	Std sales Std mix $	Diff in units	× std profit $	Variance $
X	5,150	5,000	150 (F)	8	1,200 (F)
Y	3,090	3,000	90 (F)	14	1,260 (F)
Z	2,060	2,000	60 (F)	16	960 (F)
					3,420 (F)

13.22 The correct answer is: $209,500

$210,000 + $3,000 − $5,000 + $9,000 − $7,500 = $209,500.

Budgeted profit	not required	
Sales volume variance	not needed	
Standard profit on actual sales	209,500	
Sales price variance	7,500	favourable
Total variable cost variance	9,000	adverse
Fixed cost expenditure variance	5,000	favourable
Fixed cost volume variance	3,000	adverse
Actual profit	210,000	

14 Modern business concepts

14.1 The correct answers are:

- Pull scheduling: buying or producing at each stage of the supply chain only when the next stage in the chain wants the output.

- Kanban control: using a system of signalling work flow requirements using cards or other signalling devices.

- Greater visibility of what is going on, such as open plan work place layouts and coloured lights to indicate stoppages.

JIT operations use pull scheduling, Kanban control and greater visibility in the work place. Pull scheduling (only producing for the next stage in the chain when the work is needed) results in a sacrifice of capacity utilisation. Supporters of JIT argue that it is better to be idle than to work on producing items for inventory. JIT purchasing systems rely on selecting a small number of reliable suppliers for key items, and involving these suppliers in the JIT planning and purchase ordering system.

14.2 The correct answer is:

A system which is driven by demand for finished products, whereby each component on a production line is produced only when needed for the next stage.

14.3   The correct answers are:

Cost	Classification
Repairs under warranty	B
Inspection of goods in	C
Product design	D
Lower selling price for sub quality goods	A

14.4   The correct answer is: Performance testing.

Performance testing is an appraisal cost.

Re-inspection cost is an internal failure cost. Administration of customer complaints section is an external failure cost and training in quality control is a prevention cost.

14.5   The correct answers are:

- Close relationship with suppliers.
- Minimal set up time and costs.
- Similar production time across all stages of the production process.

A close relationship with suppliers (so that raw materials are delivered as they are required), minimal set-up time and costs (so that small production runs are feasible) and similar production time of all stages of the production process (so that the speed of all processes matches the rate at which the final product is demanded by customers) are key requirements of successful JIT.

It does not matter whether raw materials are perishable or not (but if they are perishable, JIT is even more desirable).

14.6   The correct answers are:

- For standard costing to be useful for control purposes, it requires a reasonably stable environment;

- The ethos behind a system of standard costing is that performance is satisfactory if it meets predetermined standards;

- The control aspect of standard costing systems is achieved by making individual managers responsible for the variances relating to their part of the organisation's activities.

Cost and quality are important in a TQM environment.

If standards were set on an ideal basis, this would enforce the concept of continual improvement that TQM embodies.

In a standard costing environment, products or processes must be standardised and repetitive, so that standards can be established which will be useful for monitoring and control. In a total quality environment, however, continual improvements are likely to alter prices, quantities of inputs and so on.

Attainable standards, which make some allowance for waste and inefficiencies, are more common than ideal standards. The use of such standards conflicts with the elimination of waste which is a vital ingredient of a TQM programme.

14.7   The correct answers are:

- Dedicated cell production
- TQM

The CIMA *Official Terminology's* definition of WCM is a 'position of international manufacturing excellence, achieved by developing a culture based on factors such as continuous improvement, problem prevention, zero defect tolerance, customer-driven JIT-based production and total quality management.'

Absorption costing and mass production would not be associated with such aims.

14.8   The correct answers are: 'Standard costing systems cannot be used in an industry that operates in a rapidly-changing environment' is true. 'Standard costing systems are compatible with a Total Quality Management approach' and 'Standard costing is well suited to organisations that produce items to customer specifications' are false.

Standard costing systems are not compatible with a Total Quality Management approach to operations. With standard costing, the aim is to achieve standard cost or perhaps obtain some favourable variances. With TQM, guiding principles are 'continuous improvement' and 'zero defects'. Existing standards and methods of operating are always unsatisfactory and improvements should always be sought. This is not compatible with a standard costing 'philosophy'.

Standard costing is of no value in a rapidly-changing environment because products are not standardised for a sufficient length of time to make the preparation of standard costs worthwhile.

Standard costing is not well suited to production where items are made to customer specifications. This is because items are not produced to standard specifications on which a standard cost can be based.

14.9   The correct answers are:

- It is not always easy to predict patterns of demand.
- JIT makes the organisation far more vulnerable to disruptions in the supply chain.
- Wide geographical spread makes JIT difficult.

There is not a danger of inventory becoming obsolete as raw materials will only be purchased when they are needed for production and production is driven by demand for finished products. The minimal inventory levels mean that there is much less chance of obsolescence. The fact that JIT is demand led system is actually a benefit rather than a problem.

14.10 The correct answers are:

- Quality and reliability
- Flexibility
- Customer satisfaction

WCM incorporates the principles of Total Quality Management.

WCM aims to know what customer requirements are, to supply customers reliably and on time and to change products/develop new products as customer needs change.

It may be necessary to exceed the target cost and generate adverse variances to ensure that the desired level of quality and customer satisfaction are obtained.

14.11 The correct answers are:

- Administration of quality control
- Maintenance of inspection equipment
- Training in quality control

Performance testing is an appraisal cost. Costs of repair under warranty are external failure costs.

14.12 The correct answer is: $500
The oven breakdown repair is an internal failure cost of quality.

The inspection of flour is an appraisal cost. The training for staff is a prevention cost of quality. The cost of taste tests after production are also an appraisal cost.

15 Environmental costing

15.1 The correct answers are:

- Reducing energy consumption
- Increasing use of renewable electricity
- Offsetting

Using more energy from the national grid/country's central supply will actually increase the carbon consumed by the organisation.

15.2 The correct answers are:

- Cleaning up contaminated soil
- Government penalties and fines

Environmental external failure costs are costs arising when the business releases harmful waste into the environment

15.3 The correct answer is: They are both true.

A system of environmental management accounting provides environmental information for internal use by management, but not for external reporting. It is distinct from environmental accounting, which is concerned with external reporting (as well as internal reporting). Environmental management accounting systems typically make use of life cycle costing, given that there may be substantial clean-up and disposal costs at the end of the life of an activity or operation.

15.4 The correct answer is:

Physical information about the use and flows of energy, water and materials, including waste and emissions.

Environmental management accounting measures physical quantities as well as monetary amounts. Management accounting is concerned with providing information to management, not with external reporting to shareholders.

15.5 The correct answers are:

- Distinguishing the business from its competitors
- Driving down energy costs
- Improving corporate reputation

The two incorrect answers will increase the use of greenhouse gases.

This probably seems like an easy question when written in this format where you just have to tick the boxes. In the ICS exam, however, you may be asked to think of reasons why a business would benefit from reducing its greenhouse gases. You need to be able to think of these types of reasons for yourself and relate them to the particular business which is given in the question. You could use the mnemonic CREAM. Competition, Reputation, Energy savings (cost), Alternatives, Morale.

15.6 The correct answer is: $1,500

The only environmental external failure cost is the fine for carbon dioxide emissions.

Forming an environmental policy is an appraisal cost. The training for staff is a prevention cost. The monthly maintenance is also a prevention cost.

15.7 The correct answer is: $36,000

Total number of environmental inspections = [(1,500/500) × 3] + [(3,000/1,000) × 8] + [(1,600/800) × 7] = 9+24+14 = 47

Cost per inspection = $70,500 / 47 = $1,500. Cost attributed to MyRun = $1,500 × 8 × 3= $36,000

15.8   The correct answers are:

- Environmental costing leads to more accurate pricing

- Using an activity based system, environmental costs become cost drivers

Identifying environmental costs associated with individual products or services leads to more accurate costs and therefore more accurate pricing.

A problem with traditional costing methods is that they fail to analyse environmental costs and the costs are often hidden within overhead costs. They are therefore not necessarily easy to measure. One solution to this is to use activity based costing where the environmental costs become cost drivers.

Environmental costs can be classified in the same way as quality cost classification. To aid comparison, they should be expressed as a percentage of turnover (not profit) in the same way that quality costs are.

15.9   The correct answer is: $16,000

Cost per kg of hazardous waste disposed of = $40,000 / 160,000 kg = $0.25 per kg.
Cost attributed to Leaf = $0.25 × 2 × 20,000 = $10,000.
Cost per inspection = $15,000 / 150 = $100 per inspection.
Cost attributed to Leaf = $100 × 60 = $6,000.
Total cost attributed to Leaf = $10,000 + $6,000 = $16,000.

15.10 The correct answer is: They would all lead to cost savings.

The gym would expect to see reductions in all of these costs which would arise from using ABC to identify environmental costs. For example, water and electricity consumption would be reduced if the towels were washed less frequently as would the use of detergent, as these would be variable costs of running the washing machines. If the towels are washed less frequently, the assumptions are that they wouldn't wear out as quickly and fewer members of staff would be needed to work in the laundry department.

Practice mock questions

Questions

1   A regression equation Y = a + bX is used to forecast the value of Y for a given value of X.

Which THREE of the following increase the reliability of the forecast?

☐   A correlation coefficient numerically close to 1.

☐   Working to a higher number of decimal places of accuracy.

☐   Forecasting the values of X outside the range used in the sample.

☐   A large sample is used to calculate the regression equation.

☐   Forecasting the values of X within the range used in the sample.

---

2   **Write down the correct classification of each of the following quality costs.**

Cost   **Classification**

Machine maintenance   [   ]

Product recall   [   ]

Inspection of goods inwards   [   ]

Reworking faulty items   [   ]

Options:

Prevention cost
Appraisal cost
Internal failure cost
External failure cost

---

3   A manager is considering the price to charge for a new product.

The contribution depending on the level of demand and the selling price is shown in the payoff table below:

		Selling price		
Demand	$6	$7	$8	$9
High	$10,000	$12,000	$11,000	$10,500
Medium	$5,000	$6,000	$10,000	$8,000
Low	$4,000	$3,000	$8,000	$7,000

If the manager applies the maximin criterion to make decisions the selling price chosen will be:

☐ $6

☐ $7

☐ $8

☐ $9

4   **Which of the following best describes a basic standard?**

☐   A standard which is based on ideal operating conditions and makes no allowance for waste, machine break downs or other idle time.

☐   A standard which is based on current prices.

☐   A standard which is unaltered over a period of time.

☐   A standard which seeks improvement in the current operating conditions, but makes allowances for waste, machine breakdowns and other normal losses.

---

5   **Match the following activities with the most appropriate cost drivers:**

Activity/Cost pool	Cost driver
Machine repairs	
Quality control	
Receiving	
Supervisor's salary	

Choose from the following cost drivers:

Number of component receipts
Number of labour hours
Number of machine hours
Number of production runs

---

6   **If a company has no production resource limitations, in which order would the following budgets be prepared?**

☐   Production, finished goods inventory, sales, materials inventory, materials usage, materials purchases

☐   Sales, production, finished goods inventory, materials usage, materials inventory, materials purchases

☐   Sales, finished goods inventory, production, materials usage, materials inventory, materials purchases

☐   Sales, finished goods inventory, production, materials inventory, materials usage, materials purchases

---

7   Using absorption costing the profit for the year ending 31 Dec 20X4 was $67,125. The overhead absorption rate is $3 per unit. At the start of the year there were 350 units of finished goods inventory and this had risen to 475 units by the end of the year.

The profit using marginal costing is:

$ [   ]

---

8   A Co plans to sell 34,000 units of Product Q next year. Opening inventory of Q is expected to be 5,000 units and A Co plans to increase inventory by 20% by the end of the year.

The number of units of Product Q which should be produced next year is:

[   ] units

9   **What is defined as 'an activity within an organisation which has a lower capacity than preceding or subsequent activities, thereby limiting throughput'?**

☐   Constraint

☐   Limiting factor

☐   Bottleneck

☐   Principal budget factor

---

10   The following table shows the number of clients who visited a hair dressing salon in the last quarter along with the total costs incurred each month:

Month	Number of clients	Total cost
		$
January	160	10,500
February	168	10,996
March	166	10,650

Which of the following could be used to forecast total costs (where y = forecast total costs) from the number of clients expected to attend (where x = the expected number of clients)?

☐   y = 500 + 62x

☐   y = 10,500/x

☐   y = 6,500 + 25x

☐   y = 580 + 62x

---

11   **The main purpose of sensitivity analysis is to:**

☐   Predict the future outcome from an uncertain situation.

☐   Determine the outcome from a situation in the event of the worst possible outcome.

☐   Determine the expected value of an outcome that is uncertain.

☐   Gain insight into which assumptions or variables in a situation are critical.

---

12   **Which of the following is an advantage of non-participative budgeting when compared to participative budgeting?**

☐   It increases motivation.

☐   It decreases budgetary slack.

☐   It increases acceptance.

☐   The budgets produced are more likely to be achieved.

---

13   **Which THREE of the following statements about JIT are correct?**

☐   In a JIT environment there is a risk that inventory will become obsolete.

☐   JIT requires strong relationships with suppliers.

☐   JIT is difficult to implement if customer demand is uncertain.

☐   JIT increases the need for large warehouses.

☐   JIT protects an organisation against risks of disruption in the supply chain.

☐   JIT works best when suppliers are located within a narrow geographical spread.

14 The following budget was prepared by F Co at the start of the accounting period:

	Original budget
Sales units	600
	$
Sales revenue	54,000
Direct material	16,200
Direct labour	6,000
Variable overhead	3,000
Fixed overheard	15,000
Profit	13,800

If actual sales are 550 units, the flexed budgeted profit is:

☐ $8,400

☐ $11,400

☐ $12,650

☐ $13,800

15 **Which of the following could explain an adverse material usage variance?**

(i)   Purchase of cheaper materials.
(ii)   Recruitment of temporary workers.
(iii) Overtime worked by existing workers.
(iv) Purchase of better quality materials.

☐ (i) only

☐ (i) and (ii)

☐ (ii) only

☐ (iii) and (iv)

16 Six years ago Material D cost $10 per kg and the price index most appropriate to the cost of material D was 130. Now the index has risen to 510.

The best estimate of the current cost of material D per kg is:

☐ $2.55

☐ $29.23

☐ $39.23

☐ $51.00

17 P Co has over-absorbed fixed production overheads for the period by $12,000. The fixed production overhead absorption rate was $16 per unit and is based on the normal level of activity of 5,000 units. Actual production was 4,500 units.

The actual fixed production overheads incurred for the period was:

☐ $60,000

☐ $68,000

☐ $72,000

☐ $80,000

BPP
LEARNING MEDIA

18   **What is the name given to a budget which has been prepared by updating the current budget to reflect a change in economic conditions?**

    ☐   Incremental budget

    ☐   Flexible budget

    ☐   Rolling budget

    ☐   Zero based budget

---

19   **Which of the following is NOT a limitation of using expected values?**

    ☐   It ignores risk.

    ☐   It is heavily dependent on probability estimates.

    ☐   It is inappropriate for repeated decisions.

    ☐   The EV is unlikely to correspond to one of the outcomes.

---

20   XY Co is trying to decide which of four potential projects to invest in, but is concerned about risk. The following information has been obtained about the four potential projects.

Project	A	B	C	D
Expected contribution	9,000	9,000	8,000	8,000
Standard deviation	400	500	400	500

Which of the projects has the highest relative dispersion and therefore risk?

    ☐   Project A

    ☐   Project B

    ☐   Project C

    ☐   Project D

---

21   Each unit of Product Webster requires 2 kg of raw material.

Next week's production budget for Product Webster is as follows:

Opening inventories:
  Raw materials   6,000 kg
  Finished units of Webster   2,300 units
Budgeted sales of Webster   18,000 units
Planned closing inventories:
  Raw materials   5,000 kg
  Finished units of Webster   2,000 units

The quantity of raw materials to purchase for next week is:

    [   ] kg

---

22 A company manufactures four products using the same grade of labour, which is in short supply. The following budgeted data relates to the products:

	A	B	C	D
Selling price	100	110	95	90
Material A	(20)	(30)	(17)	(15)
Labour cost (@ $8 per hour)	(16)	(40)	(32)	(20)
Fixed overheads	(40)	(30)	(6)	(15)
Profit	24	30	40	40

Rank the products in the order they should be manufactured if we are seeking to maximise profits:

	1st	2nd	3rd	4th
Product A	☐	☐	☐	☐
Product B	☐	☐	☐	☐
Product C	☐	☐	☐	☐
Product D	☐	☐	☐	☐

23 B Co makes and sells a single product called the BR. In the forthcoming year it is anticipated that 2,900 units will be sold at a sales price of $90 each and a contribution to sales ratio of 30%. Management believe that the margin of safety will be 15%.

Budgeted fixed costs during the year are:

$ ☐

24 **Which of the following THREE statements about joint product costs are true?**

☐ Joint costs can be apportioned and used to value inventory.

☐ Joint costs are not relevant for further processing decisions because they are sunk costs.

☐ Joint costs are relevant if all of the joint products are being processed further.

☐ Joint costs must be apportioned based on net realisable value before the point of separation.

☐ Normal losses are valued at scrap value.

25 **Which of the following control actions could be taken to help eliminate an adverse direct labour efficiency variance?**

(i)   Employ more highly skilled labour.
(ii) Ensure stricter supervision of labour workers.
(iii) Ask employees to work paid overtime.

☐ (i) and (iii)

☐ (i) and (ii)

☐ (ii) and (iii)

☐ All of the above.

26 Camp Co is trying to predict sales of its new tent, but it will be dependent on the weather. The Sales Manager predicts that 10,000 tents will be sold if the weather is dry, but only 6,000 if the summer if wet. The probability of a dry summer is 0.3. Each tent will retail for $300.

What is the expected value of the sales revenue for the forthcoming year?

$ ☐

27 A special contract is being considered by JB Co. It will require using 400 kg of material A and 150 kg of material C.

The company currently has 200 kg of material A in inventory, which cost $10 per kg. If not used on the special contract the inventory would have to be disposed of at a cost of $0.50 per kg. The current market price of material A is $12.

40 kg of material C are in inventory and cost $15 when purchased last month. The current replacement cost is $14 and material C is in regular use for the manufacture of other products.

The relevant cost of the materials required for the special contract is:

☐ $3,000

☐ $4,400

☐ $6,500

☐ $6,900

---

28 S Co uses variance analysis to control costs and revenues.

Information concerning sales is as follows:

Budgeted sales price ($)	15 per unit
Budgeted sales volume	10,000 units
Budgeted contribution per unit ($)	7
Budgeted profit per unit ($)	5
Actual sales revenue ($)	163,000
Actual units sold	10,800 units

The sales volume profit variance is:

☐ $4,000 Favourable

☐ $5,600 Favourable

☐ $1,000 Favourable

☐ $13,000 Favourable

29   Select the appropriate term from the list below to describe A, B and C on the PV chart below:

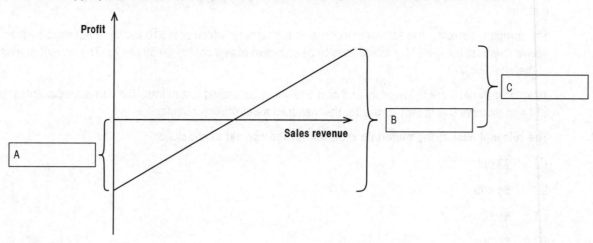

Select from:

Variable costs
Fixed costs
Profit
Contribution
Total sales revenue

30   The following details have been extracted from the receivables' records of R Co:

Invoices paid in the month of sale	25%
Invoice paid in the first month after sale	70%
Invoices paid in the second month after sale	5%

Credit sales for July to September are budgeted as follows:

July	$500,000
August	$600,000
September	$560,000

Customers who pay in the month of sale receive a settlement discount of 5%.

The budgeted amount due to be received from customers in September is:

$ [   ]

31   Fish Co makes a variety of different products, but its ability to fulfil customer demand is restricted by the availability of manufacturing hours on Machine K. There are 4,000 hours available per month. Product Gold requires 30 minutes of machine time.

The cost card for Product Gold is as follows:

	$
Selling price	50
Less: material A	(26)
Labour (2 hours @ $5)	(10)
Contribution per unit	15

What is the throughput contribution per unit of Product Gold?

$ [   ]

32   CTF Co uses activity based costing and manufactures three products called the Jay, Kay and Ell. The following information is available for 20X2:

	Jay	Kay	Ell
Budgeted production (units)	1,500	3,000	1,600
Units per batch	500	1,000	800
Number of environmental inspections per batch	3	8	7

The total cost for environmental inspections for 20X2 is expected to be $82,250.

What is the environmental cost attributed to Kay for 20X2 (to the nearest whole number)?

$ [   ]

---

33   **Put the following steps involved in an organisation's budgetary planning process into the correct order:**

	1st	2nd	3rd	4th
Form a budget committee.	☐	☐	☐	☐
Prepare the master budget and submit it to the Board for approval.	☐	☐	☐	☐
Establish the organisation's objectives.	☐	☐	☐	☐
Prepare functional budgets.	☐	☐	☐	☐

---

34   **Which THREE of the following describe the shadow price?**

    ☐   The additional contribution generated from one additional unit of limiting factor.

    ☐   The opportunity cost of not having the use of one extra unit of limiting factor.

    ☐   The binding constraint in a linear programming problem.

    ☐   The maximum amount to be paid for one additional unit of scarce resource.

    ☐   The additional contribution generated when additional units of a slack resource is made available.

    ☐   The maximum extra that should be paid for one additional unit of scarce resource.

---

35   You are asked to interpret the following extract from a decision tree, which has been prepared for a decision that is to be made to choose between D, E and F.

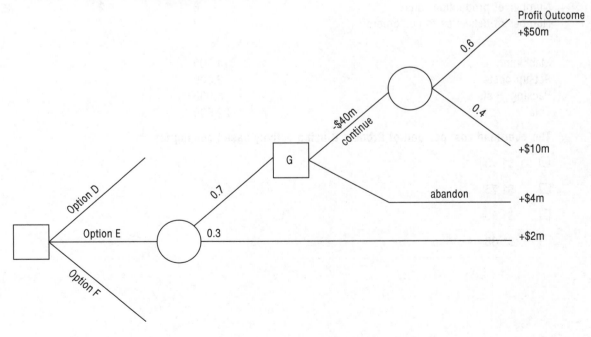

The maximum expected value of profit at decision point G is:

$ ☐ Give you answer to the nearest million.

36 The following statements have been made about full cost plus pricing.

(i) Charging prices at full cost plus a fixed margin for profit will ensure that the business will make a profit in each period.

(ii) Full cost plus pricing can lead to under and over pricing of products.

(iii) Full cost plus pricing is always preferred to marginal cost plus pricing in the short term.

Which of the above statements is/are true?

☐ (i) only

☐ (i) and (ii)

☐ (ii) only

☐ (ii) and (iii)

37 **Which THREE of the following are necessary if forecasts obtained from a time series analysis are to be reliable?**

☐ There must be no unforeseen events.

☐ The past must be a reliable indication of the future.

☐ The trend must be increasing.

☐ There must be no seasonal variation.

☐ The model used must fit the past data.

38 The following data relates to production of G Co's three products for the next year.

	Product A	Product B	Product C
Production and sales (units)	6,000	5,000	2,000
Machine hours per unit	2	3	1
Number of production runs	6	2	2
Number of deliveries to customers	8	5	7

	$
Machining	14,500
Set-up costs	2,000
Packing costs	6,000
Total	22,500

The overhead cost per unit of Product B using activity based costing is:

☐ $1.73

☐ $1.75

☐ $1.80

☐ $1.88

39   G Co makes two products – P and Q – from the same raw material. Information about the selling price and costs associated with each product are as follows:

	P $/unit	Q $/unit
Selling price	35.00	47.00
Direct material A (@ $3.50 per kg)	10.50	14.00
Direct labour	5.00	2.50
Variable overhead	2.50	1.25
Fixed overhead	7.50	3.75
Profit per unit	9.50	25.50

The maximum demand for both products is unlimited.

If material A is limited to 2,500 kg per month, the shadow price of material A is:

Give your answer to the nearest cent.

$ [   ]

---

40   BR Co combines two ingredients (A and I) to manufacture its product the BRAIN. The standard material cost and usage for each product is as follows:

		$
Material A	6 kg @ $3.00	18.00
Material I	9 kg @ $4.50	40.50
Total		58.50

In April 20X5, the actual mix used was 2,700 kg of A and 4,600 kg of I to produce 500 units of BRAIN.

The material mix variance for April 20X5 is:

☐ $330 Adverse

☐ $330 Favourable

☐ $450 Favourable

☐ $450 Adverse

---

41   **Which THREE of the following items are relevant costs?**

☐   Incremental fixed costs

☐   Apportioned fixed overheads

☐   Sunk costs

☐   Replacement cost of items held in inventory

☐   Depreciation

☐   Future cash flows

☐   Committed costs

---

42   **Which of the following is NOT an assumption of linear programming?**

☐   Fixed and variable costs are constant.

☐   Units of output are not divisible.

☐   No interdependence between products.

☐   Estimates of future demand are known with certainty.

43   K Co manufactures and sells two products – L and M. Annual fixed costs are budgeted to be $148,500 and annual sales are budgeted to be $520,000 in the ratio 2L:4M. Product L has a contribution to sales ratio of 25% and product M has a contribution to sales ratio of 37%.

The margin of safety is:

Give your answer to 1 dp.

| | %

---

44   A cleaning detergent, Sparkle, is manufactured by mixing three materials. The standard cost of manufacturing 100 litres of Sparkle is as follows:

		$
Material S	27 litres @ $1.75	47.25
Material P	55 litres @ $2.00	110.00
Material A	23 litres @ $2.20	50.60
Total		207.85

Last month 300,000 litres of Sparkle were manufactured, using 80,000 litres of S, 159,000 litres of P and 69,000 litres of A.

The material yield variance for last month is:

☐ $13,857 Adverse

☐ $13,857 Favourable

☐ $166,280 Adverse

☐ $166,280 Favourable

---

45   **Using the picklist below, select the correct order of steps for implementing zero-based budgeting.**

Rank packages | |

Define the decision packages | |

Allocate resources | |

Evaluate packages | |

Picklist

Step 1
Step 2
Step 3
Step 4

---

46   X Co is facing multiple labour constraints in the forthcoming period when it wishes to manufacture products a and b. The following constraints have been identified for labour:

Skilled labour $2a + 3b \leq 1,200$ hours

Semi-skilled labour $4a + 2b \leq 2,000$ hours

What is the maximum number of each product which could be made if there is unlimited demand for each product and no material or machine constraints?

☐   100 units of a; 450 units of b.

☐   450 units of a; 100 units of b.

☐   400 units of a; 100 units of b.

☐   100 units of a; 400 units of b.

47   A factory's entire machine capacity is used to produce essential components. The costs of using the machines are as follows:

	$
Variable costs	5,000
Fixed costs	10,000
Total costs	15,000

If all of the components were purchased from an outside supplier, the machine could be used to produce other products which would earn a total contribution of $12,000.

The maximum price that the company should be willing to pay the external supplier for the components is:

$ [   ]

---

48   **Improvements in product design or specification to reduce defective products is an example of which quality cost?**

☐   Prevention cost

☐   Appraisal cost

☐   Internal failure cost

☐   External failure cost

---

49   The standard direct material cost for MPQ's product is:

6 kg @ $8 per kg = $48.00

During October production was 7,400 units of the product and the actual materials cost was $397,400 for 45,100 kg of material.

However, it was found that due to an increase in the World price of material it should have been $8.50 per kg for the entire month, whilst at the same time new legislation stated that the product should contain 10% less ingredients for health and safety reasons.

The adverse material price planning variance for October is:

$ [   ]

---

50   Y Co is preparing a quote for a special one off contract which requires 100 hours of skilled and 50 hours of unskilled labour. Skilled labour is paid $14 per hour and unskilled labour is paid $11 per hour.

Currently skilled labour is fully utilised manufacturing Product T. Each product T requires 5 skilled labour hours and yields a contribution per unit of $30.

Semi-skilled labour has 40 hours of idle time and unlike the skilled labour, has capacity for 50 hours of overtime per month. Overtime can be worked at a rate of time and a half.

The total relevant cost of labour to include in the contract is:

$ [   ]

51 Garden Co runs a chain of garden centres and is considering opening a café at its main garden centre. The cost of refurbishing an underutilised area will be $300,000. Market research has been undertaken to predict likely interest from customers. It is anticipated that 30% of customers would use the café and current customer numbers are on average 500 per day. The garden centre is open for 360 days per year. The research has also highlighted uncertainty over the average contribution per customer. There is a 35% chance of $5, 50% chance of $7 and 15% chance of $10. Fixed costs will be negligible as staff will be relocated from elsewhere in the garden centre.

The likely contribution in the first year is:

$ [   ]

---

52 The following data relate to Product X:

	Per unit
Selling price	$10
Material cost	$2
Labour cost	$3
Overhead cost	$1.50
Time on bottleneck resource	13 minutes

Using throughput accounting, the contribution per hour for Product X is:

☐ $16.00

☐ $16.15

☐ $23.07

☐ $36.92

---

53 The following data relate to Product F for November:

	Budget	Actual
Labour rate per hour	$16.00	$18.00
Labour hours per unit	3.00	2.75
Output (units)	450.00	425.00

It has now been agreed that the standard rate per labour hour for labour worked in November should have been $17.50.

The labour rate planning variance for November is:

☐ $675 Adverse

☐ $1,912.50 Adverse

☐ $2,025 Adverse

☐ $2,550 Adverse

---

54 The following extract is taken from the production cost budget of Y Co.

Production (units)	3,000	5,000
Production cost ($)	78,000	118,000

The budgeted cost allowance for an activity level of 4,000 units is:

$ [   ]

55 A Co is preparing its production plan for next week and has estimated that there will only be 1,000 kg of material available. Demand from customers is unlimited and labour can work overtime if necessary to meet production demand.

Product	B	C	D	E
Sales price	100	120	80	120
Variable costs:				
Labour	20	30	15	40
Material A ($2/kg)	10	20	40	20
Fixed costs	50	20	20	70
Profit per unit	20	50	5	30

Which product should A Co produce next week?

☐ B

☐ C

☐ D

☐ E

---

56 A company has produced a payoff table showing the profit earned depending upon the number of units produced and the number of units demanded of a new product.

Payoff table

	Production		
Demand	*300*	*325*	*350*
300	$30,000	$27,000	$25,000
325	$30,000	$32,500	$29,000
350	$30,000	$32,500	$35,000

It has started to produce a minimax regret matrix table but there are some entries outstanding.

Complete the minimax regret matrix by selecting the appropriate figures from the list below.

	Production		
Demand	*300*	*325*	*350*
300	$0		
325	$2,500	$0	
350	$5,000		

Picklist

$5,000
$3,500
$2,500
$3,000
$0

---

57 A company's budget for the next period shows that it would breakeven at sales revenue of $600,000 and fixed costs of $240,000.

The sales revenue needed to achieve a profit of $180,000 in the next period is:

$ [   ]

BPP
LEARNING MEDIA

58 A production process produces two joint products and each of the products can be sold immediately after the process or further processed individually before being sold. The following process account relates to last month's production:

PROCESS

	Units	$		Units	$
Materials	2,000	26,000			
Labour		4,000	Product A	800	12,600
Variable overhead		1,500	Product B	1,200	18,900
	2,000	31,500		2,000	31,500

Each of the products can be sold immediately after the process or further processed individually before being sold.

Product	Selling price after process $/Unit	Selling price after further processing $/Unit	Further variable processing cost $/Unit
A	16	19	3.15
B	20	24	3.75

Using relevant costing principles which of the following courses of action should be recommended for the company?

☐ Process A and B further.

☐ Process A further and sell B at the point of separation.

☐ Process B further and sell A at the point of separation.

☐ Sell A and B at the point of separation.

59 The Directors of F Co are considering employing a sales manager to improve its profitability. The company is currently expecting to make $300,000 profit in the forthcoming year. Market research has shown that an excellent sales manager can increase profit by 40%, an average one by 30% and a poor one by 15%. Based on past experience the company will only be able to attract an excellent sales manager 10% of the time, an average one 50% of the time and a poor one on 40% of occasions. The sales manager would be paid $80,000 per annum regardless of ability.

Which of the following represents the best advice to the Directors of F Co?

☐ Employ a sales manager as profits are expected to increase by $75,000.

☐ Employ a sales manager as profits are expected to increase by $12,500.

☐ Do not employ a sales manager as profits would be expected to fall by $5,000.

☐ Do not employ a sales manager as profits would be expected to fall by $62,500.

60   A linear programming model has been formulated for two products, K and L. The objective function for this model is $Z = 4K + 7L$, when Z = contribution, K = the number of units of Product K to manufacture and L = the number of units of Product L to manufacture.

Material F is one of the resources constrained in the forthcoming period. Each unit of K uses 7 kg and each unit of L uses 10 kg of material. The standard costs of each kg of material F is $5 and the shadow price has been calculated as $5.90 per kg.

If an extra 25 kg of material F becomes available at $5 per kg, the maximum increase in contribution will be:

☐   Increase of $22.50

☐   Increase of $147.50

☐   Increase of $272.50

☐   No change

Practice mock answers

Answers

1   The correct answer is:

- A correlation coefficient numerically close to 1.
- A large sample is used to calculate the regression equation.
- Forecasting the values of X within the range used in the sample.

A correlation coefficient close to +1 or -1 indicates a strong linear relationship between X and Y. The regression equation is therefore more reliable for forecasting.

Working to a high number of decimal places gives spurious accuracy unless the data itself is accurate to the same degree.

Extrapolation, or forecasting the values of X outside the range used in the sample will lead to unreliable estimates as there is no evidence that the same regression relationships hold for such values.

The regression equation is worthless unless a sufficiently large sample was used to calculate it. In practice, samples of about ten or more are acceptable.

---

2   The correct answers are:

Cost	Classification
Machine maintenance	Prevention cost
Product recall	External failure cost
Inspection of goods inwards	Appraisal cost
Reworking faulty items	Internal failure cost

Maintaining machinery should ensure that unscheduled disruption and breakdowns are less likely to occur. Inspecting goods before they are used in the production process should mean that items produced are not substandard because of lower grade inputs. Reworking faulty items is classified as an internal cost as the assumption is that the problem is identified before the goods are sent to the customer. A product recall is an external failure cost as the goods are in the ownership of customers, who will become aware of the defects in the product as a result of the recall.

---

3   The correct answer is: $8.

Maximin = maximise the minimum achievable profit. The minimum achievable profits are when the demand is low. The maximum profit when demand is low is achieved when the selling price is $8.

---

4   The correct answer is:

A standard which is unaltered over a period of time.

A standard which is based on ideal operating conditions and makes no allowance for waste, machine break downs or other idle time is known as an ideal standard.

A standard which seeks improvement in the current operating conditions, but makes allowances for waste, machine breakdowns and other normal losses is known as an attainable standard.

A standard which is based on current prices is known as a current standard.

5   The correct answers are:

Activity/Cost pool	Cost driver
Machine repairs	Number of machine hours
Quality control	Number of production runs
Receiving	Number of component receipts
Supervisor's salary	Number of labour hours

The aim is to identify the cost driver that is going to cause the costs to rise. For example, if more labour hours are required the assumption is that more supervision will be required.

6   The correct answer is: Sales, finished goods inventory, production, materials usage, materials inventory, materials purchases

As there are no production resource limitations, sales would be the principal budget factor and the sales budget would be prepared first. 'Following on from this, budgeted inventory changes included in the finished goods budget would inform the number of units to produce'. From the production budget it is possible to work out the amount of material required for production, which must be adjusted for changes in material inventory to arrive at the material purchases budget.

7   The correct answer is: $66,750.

	$
Profit under AC	67,125
Change in inventory × OAR (475 – 350) × $3	375
MC profit	66,750

As inventory has increased the absorption costing profit is higher than the marginal costing profit.

8   The correct answer is: 35,000 units.

	Units
Required for sales	34,000
Required to increase inventory (5,000 × 0.2)	1,000
Total	35,000

9   The correct answer is: Bottleneck.

This is the CIMA official terminology definition of a bottleneck. When a throughput accounting approach is used the organisation will aim to elevate the bottleneck in order to increase throughput.

10   The correct answer is: y = 580 + 62x.

Using the high-low method.

Month	Number of clients	Total cost
		$
High	168	10,996
Low	160	10,500
Difference	8	495

Variable costs = 495/8 = $62

Substitute into the highest equation to find total costs:

$10,996 = fixed costs + ($62 × 168)

Fixed costs = $580

11   The correct answer is:

- Gain insight into which assumptions or variables in a situation are critical.

Sensitivity analysis can be used to identify how much the outcome from a situation or decision would be different if the value of an input variable changes. This enables identification of the most critical assumptions, as these are the ones which can afford to change least.

12   The correct answer is: It decreases budgetary slack.

Employees who participate in the budget setting process are more likely to incorporate budgetary slack than those who have budgets imposed on them. All of the other items are advantages of participative budgeting.

13   The correct answer is:

- JIT requires strong relationships with suppliers.
- JIT is difficult to implement if customer demand is uncertain.
- JIT works best when suppliers are located within a narrow geographical spread.

Inventory should not become obsolete because it is purchased as needed for production, similarly less warehouse space will be needed because of the reduction in inventory levels. An organisation is not however protected from the risks of disruption in the supply chain because it does not have any buffer inventory if supply cannot be maintained.

When demand is hard to predict it becomes more difficult to operate a demand driven operation. JIT requires flexibility which is achieved through strong supplier relationships and a smaller geographical spread.

14   The correct answer is: $11,400.

	Original budget	Per unit	Flexed amount
Sales units	600		550
	$	$	
Sales revenue	54,000	90	49,500
Direct material	16,200	27	14,850
Direct labour	6,000	10	5,500
Variable overhead	3,000	5	2,750
Fixed overhead	15,000	N/A	15,000
Profit	13,800		11,400

Alternatively, you could calculate the contribution per unit: $90 - 27 - 10 - 5 = 48.

Total flexed contribution: $48 \times 550 =$	$26,400
Less fixed costs	(15,000)
Flexed profit	11,400

15   The correct answer is: (i) and (ii).

Cheaper materials may be lower quality, which could mean that more is used and that more labour time is required because items have to be reworked due to poorer quality inputs.

Recruitment of temporary workers may also increase the amount of materials used because they are unfamiliar with the production process so use more materials.

Better quality materials are more likely to result in a favourable material usage variance and the use of overtime is not likely to affect material usage.

16   The correct answer is: $39.23.

$10 \times (510/130) = 39.23

17   The correct answer is: $60,000.

		$
FOH absorbed	$16 × 4,500	72,000
Actual FOH β	β	60,000
Over absorption		12,000

---

18   The correct answer is: Rolling budget.

A budget that is periodically updated for known changes since the original budget was set is known as a rolling budget or a continual budget.

---

19   The correct answer is: It is inappropriate for repeated decisions.

EVs are most suited for repeated decisions, in fact they are not suitable for one-off decisions because the calculation produces a long-run average, which means that the EV calculated is unlikely to be one of the possible outcomes.

All of the other options are limitations of using EVs. Risk is ignored because the spread of outcomes from the EV is not considered when EVs are used in isolation. The technique is very heavily dependent on the probabilities used, even a small change will affect the calculation.

---

20   The correct answer is: Project D.

Dispersion is measured via the coefficient of variation calculation.

$$\text{Coefficient of variation} = \frac{\text{standard deviation}}{\text{EV}}$$

Project	A	B	C	D
Expected contribution	9,000	9,000	8,000	8,000
Standard deviation	400	500	400	500
Coefficient of variation	0.0444	0.0555	0.05	0.0625

---

21   The correct answer is: 34,400 kg.

Sales	18,000
Less opening inventory	(2,300)
Plus closing inventory	2,000
Production	17,700 units
Required for production @ 2 kg per unit	35,400 kg
Less opening inventory of raw materials	(6,000)
Plus closing inventory of raw materials	5,000
Total	34,400 kg

---

22   The correct answer are:

Product A – 1st
Product B – 4th
Product C – 3rd
Product D – 2nd

Workings:

	A	B	C	D
Selling price	100	110	95	90
Material A	(20)	(30)	(17)	(15)
Labour cost (@ $8 per hour)	(16)	(40)	(32)	(20)
Contribution per unit	64	40	46	55
Labour hours per unit	2	5	4	2.5
Contribution per labour hour	32	8	11.5	22
Rank	1	4	3	2

23   The correct answer is: $66,555

$$\text{MoS} = \frac{(\text{Budgeted sales} - \text{Breakeven sales})}{\text{Budgeted Sales}}$$

$$0.15 = \frac{(2,900 - \text{Breakeven sales})}{2,900} = 2,465 \text{ units}$$

Breakeven Revenue = 2,465 × $90 = $221,850

$$\text{Breakeven Revenue} = \frac{\text{Fixed costs}}{\text{C/S ratio}}$$

$$\$221,850 = \frac{\text{Fixed costs}}{0.3}$$

Therefore budgeted fixed costs = $66,555

---

24   The correct answer is:

- Joint costs can be apportioned and used to value inventory.
- Joint costs are not relevant for further processing decisions because they are sunk costs.
- Normal losses are valued at scrap value.

Joint costs are used to assess the viability of the common process, this can be done regardless of whether all or some of the products are being processed further.

Joint costs can be apportioned based on net realisable value before the point of separation, but this is not the only method. For example physical quantity or relative sales value could also be used.

---

25   The correct answer is: (i) and (ii).

An adverse labour efficiency variance means that employees are taking longer than the standard time to produce the products. Employing more highly skilled labour should help to speed up the process meaning that statement (i) is true. Increased supervision should also mean that less time is wasted, so statement (ii) is also true. Asking employees to work paid overtime may actually make the situation worse, as employees may slow down further in order to earn extra wages. Therefore the final statement is false.

---

26   The correct answer is: $2,160,000.

Workings

EV units: (10,000 × 0.3) + (6,000 × 0.7) = 7,200 units

Sales revenue = Sales volume × Selling price = 7,200 × $300 = $2,160,000.

---

27   The correct answer is: $4,400.

Workings

		$
Material A		
200 kg in inventory – saved disposal costs	(200 × $0.5)	(100)
200 kg required to purchase at current market price	(200 × $12)	2,400
Material C		
150 kg at current market price (as in constant use)	(150 × 14)	2,100
Total		4,400

28   The correct answer is: $4,000 Favourable.

Sales volume variance.

	Units
Budgeted sales volume	10,000
Actual sales volume	10,800
Difference	800
Valued @ standard profit per unit ($5)	$4,000 Favourable

29   The correct answers are:

A = Fixed costs
B = Contribution
C = Profit

30   The correct answer is: $578,000

		$
July	$500,000 × 0.05	25,000
August	$600,000 × 0.7	420,000
September	$560,000 × 0.25 × 0.95	133,000
Total		578,000

31   The correct answer is: $24.

Throughput contribution per unit = selling price per unit less material cost per unit.

$50 − $26 = $24

32   The correct answer is: $42,000

Total number of environmental inspections = [(1,500/500) × 3] + [(3,000/1,000) × 8] + [(1,600/800) × 7]
= 9 + 24 + 14 = 47

Cost per inspection = $82,250 / 47 = $1,750. Cost attributed to Kay = $1,750 × 8 × 3 = $42,000

33

Establish the organisation's objectives.	1st
Form a budget committee.	2nd
Prepare functional budgets.	3rd
Prepare the master budget and submit it to the Board for approval.	4th

34   The correct answers are:

- The additional contribution generated from one additional unit of limiting factor.
- The opportunity cost of not having the use of one extra unit of limiting factor.
- The maximum extra that should be paid for one additional unit of scarce resource.

A slack resource by definition is not a binding constraint and therefore a premium would not be paid to obtain more. A binding constraint in a linear programming problem will have a shadow price, but being binding does not define the shadow price.

The additional contribution generated when additional units of a slack resource is made available is not true because the shadow price is the extra contribution from ONE additional unit rather than additional units.

---

35   The correct answer is: 4.

Workings

EV if continue = (50 × 0.6) + (10 × 0.4) − 40 = −6

EV if abandon = 4

Therefore choose to abandon at point G, as this is the highest EV.

---

36   The correct answer is: (ii) only.

The allocation and apportionment of overheads between products can be fairly arbitrary in nature, with the result that some products have a high overhead cost and others a low overhead cost. This will affect prices, and depending on market conditions, could result in prices that are too high to attract customers, or too low (so that demand may exceed output).

Charging prices at full cost plus a fixed margin for profit will not necessarily ensure that the business will make a profit in each period. Profitability will also depend on working at or close to budgeted capacity, otherwise there could be substantial 'losses' from under-absorbed fixed overheads.

Fixed overheads are not relevant for short-term decisions, as a result marginal cost plus pricing is usually preferred to full cost plus pricing in the short term.

---

37   The correct answers are:

- There must be no unforeseen events.
- The past must be a reliable indication of the future.
- The model used must fit the past data.

Explanations: There must be no unforeseen events – we assume that there is no random or cyclical variation.

The past must be a reliable indication of the future – the assumption made in forecasting is that everything continues as in the past, for example there are no changes in the business model.

The trend must be increasing – this does not necessarily affect the reliability of the results if the multiplicative model is used. There must be no seasonal variation – not true provided that the seasonal variation observed historically continues in to the future.

The model used must fit the past data – if the model used is inappropriate, for example using an additive model when the trend is changing sharply will not be very reliable.

38   The correct answers is: $1.88.

	Driver	OAR	For Product B
Machining	Machine hours	(14,500 / ((6000 × 2) + (5,000 × 3) + 2000) = $0.5 per machine hour	$0.5 × 15,000 hours = $7,500
Set-up costs	Production runs	2,000 / 10 = $200 per set up	$200 × 2 set ups = $400
Packing costs	Deliveries	6,000 / 20 = $300 per delivery	$300 × 5 deliveries = $1,500
Total			$9,400
Per unit			$9,400/5,000 = $1.88

---

39   The correct answer is: $7.31.

The shadow price represents the extra contribution from one more unit of scarce resource.

	P	Q
	$/unit	$/unit
Selling price	35.00	47.00
Direct material A (@ $3.50 per kg)	10.50	14.00
Direct labour	5.00	2.50
Variable overhead	2.50	1.25
Contribution per unit	17.00	29.25
Material A per unit kg	3	4
Contribution per kg	5.67	7.31
Rank	2	1

---

40   The correct answer is: $330 Adverse.

Material	Actual usage in actual mix	Actual usage in standard mix	Difference	Standard cst $	Variance $
A	2,700	2,920 (w1)	220	3.00	660 (F)
I	4,600	4,380 (w2)	220	4.50	990 (A)
	7,300	7,300			330 (A)

W1

(6/15) × 7,300 kg = 2,920

W2

(9/15) × 7,300 kg = 4,380

---

41   The correct answer is:

- Incremental fixed costs.
- Future cash flows.
- Replacement cost of items held in inventory.

A relevant cost is defined as a future incremental cash flow, this means that it must involve a future cash outlay by the business. This could be in the form of incremental fixed overheads, or additional variable costs, such as the replacement of items held in inventory.

It will never include notional amounts such as depreciation, or overheads which would be incurred anyway (apportioned fixed overheads). It will also exclude committed costs as the organisation would have to pay these regardless and sunk costs as these have already been paid.

---

42   The correct answer is: Units of output are not divisible.

As linear programming is a mathematical model it assumes that resources can be combined to produce parts of a unit. Clearly in most cases it would not be appropriate to start manufacturing a unit which could not be finished, but this is one of the limitations of the technique.

The other assumptions are also limitations of the technique as in reality costs are rarely constant and it is unlikely that there would not be interdependence between products or that future demand could be accurately predicted.

---

43   The correct answer is: 13.5%

$$MoS = \frac{(\text{Budgeted sales} - \text{Breakeven sales})}{\text{Budgeted sales}}$$

Therefore need to calculate the Breakeven sales revenue: Fixed costs/Weighted average CS ratio.

$$\text{Weighted average CS ratio} = \frac{(2 \times 25) + (4 \times 37)}{6} = 33\%$$

Breakeven sales revenue = 148,500/0.33 + $450,000

$$MoS = \frac{(520,000 - 450,000)}{520,000} = 0.1346 = 13.5\%$$

---

44   The correct answer is $13,857 Favourable.

Total inputs = 80,000 + 159,000 + 69,000 = 308,000.

308,000 should yield @ (100/105) [remembering to take losses into consideration] =	239,333 litres
Did yield	300,000 litres
Difference	6,667 litres
Valued @ standard cost per litre ($207.85/100)	$13,857 Favourable

The alternative calculation of yield variance is not recommended when loses occur during the production process.

---

45   Step 1   Define the decision packages

Step 2   Evaluate packages

Step 3   Rank packages

Step 4   Allocate resources

This is the process of ZBB, which may seem straightforward but can be difficult to implement in reality.

---

46   The correct answer is: 450 units of a; 100 units of b.

Need to solve the two constraints using simultaneous equations.

(1) 2a + 3b = 1,200

(2) 4a + 2b = 2,000

Multiply equation (1) by 2, so that both equations contain 4a

(1a) 4a + 6b   = 2,400

Take equation (2) from (1a)

4b	= 400
b	= 100
Substitute b	= 100 into equation (2)
4a + (2 × 100)	= 2,000
4a	= 1,800
a	= 450

47   The correct answer is: $17,000.

	$
Variable costs saved	5,000
Contribution from using the machine	12,000
Total prepared to pay	17,000

The fixed costs are not considered as these will be incurred regardless of what the machine is used for. The contribution from using the machine to manufacture another product will be relevant because this can only occur if the components are outsourced, this is known as an opportunity cost.

48   The correct answer is:

- Prevention cost – prevention costs are incurred prior to, or during production in order to prevent or reduce product defects.

49   The correct answer is: $19,980 Adverse.

		$
Actual production @ revised usage @ standard cost	7,400 units × 5.4 kg × $8	319,680
Actual production @ revised usage @ revised costs	7,400 units × 5.4 kg × $8.50	339,660
Difference		19,980 Adverse

50   The correct answer is: $2,165.

		$
Skilled labour		
Lost contribution from	$30/5 = $6 per hour	600
Product T	× 100 hours	
Variable cost of skilled labour	100 hours × $14	1,400
Unskilled labour		
Unskilled labour – 40 hours of spare capacity		Nil
Unskilled labour overtime	10 hours × $11 × 1.5	165
Total		2,165

51   The correct answer is: $364,500.

Workings:

Expected number of customers per year: 500 × 0.3 × 360 = 54,000

Expected contribution per customer: (0.35 × $5) + (0.5 × $7) (0.15 × $10) = $6.75

Expected contribution per year: $6.75 × 54,000 = $364,500

The refurbishment costs have been excluded as these would form part of the profit calculation.

52   The correct answer is: $36.92.

Contribution per hour = throughput contribution per unit/time per unit on scarce resource

$$= (10 - 2)/(13/60)$$

$$= \$36.92$$

53   The correct answer is: $1,912.50 Adverse.

		$
Actual production @ revised usage @ standard cost	425 units × 3 hours × $16	20,400.00
Actual production @ revised usage @ revised costs	425 units × 3 hours × $17.50	22,312.50
Difference		1,912.50 Adverse

54   The correct answer is: $98,000.

Using the high-low method:

	Production (units)	Production cost ($)
High	5,000	118,000
Low	3,000	78,000
Difference	2,000	40,000

Variable cost = 40,000 / 2,000 = $20 per unit

Substitute into high equation to find fixed costs

$118,000   = fixed costs + ($20 × 5,000)

Fixed costs   = $18,000

Y = 18,000 + 20X, when X = 4,000

Y = 18,000 + (20 × 4,000) = $98,000

---

55   The correct answer is: B

Product	B	C	D	E
Sales price	100	120	80	120
Variable costs:				
Labour	20	30	15	40
Material A ($2/kg)	10	20	40	20
Contribution	70	70	25	60
Kg of material per unit	5	10	20	10
Contribution per kg	14	7	1.25	6
Rank	1	2	4	3

Remember not to include the fixed costs when making a limiting factor decision, as in this example product C would have been the preferred option.

---

56   The correct answer is:

		Production	
Demand	300	325	350
300	$0	$3,000	$5,000
325	$2,500	$0	$3,500
350	$5,000	$2,500	$0

The values in a minimax regret table represent the opportunity cost of having chosen the wrong level of production for the actual level of demand.

---

57   The correct answer is: $1,050,000.

Workings

$$\text{BE sales revenue} = \frac{\text{Fixed cost}}{\text{C/S ratio}} = 600{,}000 = \frac{240{,}000}{\text{C/S ratio}}$$

Therefore the C/S ratio = 0.4

$$\text{Therefore the C/S ratio} = \frac{\text{Fixed cost} + \text{target profit}}{\text{C/S ratio}} = \frac{240{,}000 + 180{,}000}{0.4}$$

$$= \$1{,}050{,}000$$

---

58   The correct answer is: Process B further and sell A at the point of separation.

Product	Selling price after process $/Unit	Selling price after further processing $/Unit	Incremental revenue if process further $/Unit	Further variable processing cost $/Unit	Profit or loss if processed further $/Unit
A	16	19	3	3.15	(0.15)
B	20	24	4	3.75	0.25

59   The correct answer is:

- Do not employ a sales manager as profits would be expected to fall by $5,000.

Workings

Manager	New profit before salary considered	Probability of occurring	EV $'000s
Excellent	$300,000 × 1.4 = $420,00	0.1	42
Average	$300,000 × 1.3 = $390,000	0.5	195
Poor	$300,000 × 1.15 - $345,000	0.4	138
Total			375
Less current forecast profit			(300)
Less Sales Manager's salary			(80)
Reduction in profit			(5)

60   The correct answer is: Increase of $147.50.

The shadow price represents the additional contribution which can be earned if one more unit of scarce resource is available, this has been calculated as $5.90 per kg. Since 25 extra kg are available the maximum extra contribution is 25 × $5.90 = $147.50.

Mathematical tables

PRESENT VALUE TABLE

Present value of 1.00 unit of currency, that is $(1+r)^{-n}$ where r = interest rate; n = number of periods until payment or receipt.

Periods (n)	Interest rates (r)									
	1%	2%	3%	4%	5%	6%	7%	8%	9%	10%
1	0.990	0.980	0.971	0.962	0.952	0.943	0.935	0.926	0.917	0.909
2	0.980	0.961	0.943	0.925	0.907	0.890	0.873	0.857	0.842	0.826
3	0.971	0.942	0.915	0.889	0.864	0.840	0.816	0.794	0.772	0.751
4	0.961	0.924	0.888	0.855	0.823	0.792	0.763	0.735	0.708	0.683
5	0.951	0.906	0.863	0.822	0.784	0.747	0.713	0.681	0.650	0.621
6	0.942	0.888	0.837	0.790	0.746	0.705	0.666	0.630	0.596	0.564
7	0.933	0.871	0.813	0.760	0.711	0.665	0.623	0.583	0.547	0.513
8	0.923	0.853	0.789	0.731	0.677	0.627	0.582	0.540	0.502	0.467
9	0.914	0.837	0.766	0.703	0.645	0.592	0.544	0.500	0.460	0.424
10	0.905	0.820	0.744	0.676	0.614	0.558	0.508	0.463	0.422	0.386
11	0.896	0.804	0.722	0.650	0.585	0.527	0.475	0.429	0.388	0.350
12	0.887	0.788	0.701	0.625	0.557	0.497	0.444	0.397	0.356	0.319
13	0.879	0.773	0.681	0.601	0.530	0.469	0.415	0.368	0.326	0.290
14	0.870	0.758	0.661	0.577	0.505	0.442	0.388	0.340	0.299	0.263
15	0.861	0.743	0.642	0.555	0.481	0.417	0.362	0.315	0.275	0.239
16	0.853	0.728	0.623	0.534	0.458	0.394	0.339	0.292	0.252	0.218
17	0.844	0.714	0.605	0.513	0.436	0.371	0.317	0.270	0.231	0.198
18	0.836	0.700	0.587	0.494	0.416	0.350	0.296	0.250	0.212	0.180
19	0.828	0.686	0.570	0.475	0.396	0.331	0.277	0.232	0.194	0.164
20	0.820	0.673	0.554	0.456	0.377	0.312	0.258	0.215	0.178	0.149

Periods (n)	Interest rates (r)									
	11%	12%	13%	14%	15%	16%	17%	18%	19%	20%
1	0.901	0.893	0.885	0.877	0.870	0.862	0.855	0.847	0.840	0.833
2	0.812	0.797	0.783	0.769	0.756	0.743	0.731	0.718	0.706	0.694
3	0.731	0.712	0.693	0.675	0.658	0.641	0.624	0.609	0.593	0.579
4	0.659	0.636	0.613	0.592	0.572	0.552	0.534	0.516	0.499	0.482
5	0.593	0.567	0.543	0.519	0.497	0.476	0.456	0.437	0.419	0.402
6	0.535	0.507	0.480	0.456	0.432	0.410	0.390	0.370	0.352	0.335
7	0.482	0.452	0.425	0.400	0.376	0.354	0.333	0.314	0.296	0.279
8	0.434	0.404	0.376	0.351	0.327	0.305	0.285	0.266	0.249	0.233
9	0.391	0.361	0.333	0.308	0.284	0.263	0.243	0.225	0.209	0.194
10	0.352	0.322	0.295	0.270	0.247	0.227	0.208	0.191	0.176	0.162
11	0.317	0.287	0.261	0.237	0.215	0.195	0.178	0.162	0.148	0.135
12	0.286	0.257	0.231	0.208	0.187	0.168	0.152	0.137	0.124	0.112
13	0.258	0.229	0.204	0.182	0.163	0.145	0.130	0.116	0.104	0.093
14	0.232	0.205	0.181	0.160	0.141	0.125	0.111	0.099	0.088	0.078
15	0.209	0.183	0.160	0.140	0.123	0.108	0.095	0.084	0.079	0.065
16	0.188	0.163	0.141	0.123	0.107	0.093	0.081	0.071	0.062	0.054
17	0.170	0.146	0.125	0.108	0.093	0.080	0.069	0.060	0.052	0.045
18	0.153	0.130	0.111	0.095	0.081	0.069	0.059	0.051	0.044	0.038
19	0.138	0.116	0.098	0.083	0.070	0.060	0.051	0.043	0.037	0.031
20	0.124	0.104	0.087	0.073	0.061	0.051	0.043	0.037	0.031	0.026

Cumulative present value of 1.00 unit of currency per annum, Receivable or Payable at the end of each year for n years $\frac{1-(1+r)^{-n}}{r}$

Periods	Interest rates (r)									
(n)	1%	2%	3%	4%	5%	6%	7%	8%	9%	10%
1	0.990	0.980	0.971	0.962	0.952	0.943	0.935	0.926	0.917	0.909
2	1.970	1.942	1.913	1.886	1.859	1.833	1.808	1.783	1.759	1.736
3	2.941	2.884	2.829	2.775	2.723	2.673	2.624	2.577	2.531	2.487
4	3.902	3.808	3.717	3.630	3.546	3.465	3.387	3.312	3.240	3.170
5	4.853	4.713	4.580	4.452	4.329	4.212	4.100	3.993	3.890	3.791
6	5.795	5.601	5.417	5.242	5.076	4.917	4.767	4.623	4.486	4.355
7	6.728	6.472	6.230	6.002	5.786	5.582	5.389	5.206	5.033	4.868
8	7.652	7.325	7.020	6.733	6.463	6.210	5.971	5.747	5.535	5.335
9	8.566	8.162	7.786	7.435	7.108	6.802	6.515	6.247	5.995	5.759
10	9.471	8.983	8.530	8.111	7.722	7.360	7.024	6.710	6.418	6.145
11	10.368	9.787	9.253	8.760	8.306	7.887	7.499	7.139	6.805	6.495
12	11.255	10.575	9.954	9.385	8.863	8.384	7.943	7.536	7.161	6.814
13	12.134	11.348	10.635	9.986	9.394	8.853	8.358	7.904	7.487	7.103
14	13.004	12.106	11.296	10.563	9.899	9.295	8.745	8.244	7.786	7.367
15	13.865	12.849	11.938	11.118	10.380	9.712	9.108	8.559	8.061	7.606
16	14.718	13.578	12.561	11.652	10.838	10.106	9.447	8.851	8.313	7.824
17	15.562	14.292	13.166	12.166	11.274	10.477	9.763	9.122	8.544	8.022
18	16.398	14.992	13.754	12.659	11.690	10.828	10.059	9.372	8.756	8.201
19	17.226	15.679	14.324	13.134	12.085	11.158	10.336	9.604	8.950	8.365
20	18.046	16.351	14.878	13.590	12.462	11.470	10.594	9.818	9.129	8.514

Periods	Interest rates (r)									
(n)	11%	12%	13%	14%	15%	16%	17%	18%	19%	20%
1	0.901	0.893	0.885	0.877	0.870	0.862	0.855	0.847	0.840	0.833
2	1.713	1.690	1.668	1.647	1.626	1.605	1.585	1.566	1.547	1.528
3	2.444	2.402	2.361	2.322	2.283	2.246	2.210	2.174	2.140	2.106
4	3.102	3.037	2.974	2.914	2.855	2.798	2.743	2.690	2.639	2.589
5	3.696	3.605	3.517	3.433	3.352	3.274	3.199	3.127	3.058	2.991
6	4.231	4.111	3.998	3.889	3.784	3.685	3.589	3.498	3.410	3.326
7	4.712	4.564	4.423	4.288	4.160	4.039	3.922	3.812	3.706	3.605
8	5.146	4.968	4.799	4.639	4.487	4.344	4.207	4.078	3.954	3.837
9	5.537	5.328	5.132	4.946	4.772	4.607	4.451	4.303	4.163	4.031
10	5.889	5.650	5.426	5.216	5.019	4.833	4.659	4.494	4.339	4.192
11	6.207	5.938	5.687	5.453	5.234	5.029	4.836	4.656	4.486	4.327
12	6.492	6.194	5.918	5.660	5.421	5.197	4.988	4.793	4.611	4.439
13	6.750	6.424	6.122	5.842	5.583	5.342	5.118	4.910	4.715	4.533
14	6.982	6.628	6.302	6.002	5.724	5.468	5.229	5.008	4.802	4.611
15	7.191	6.811	6.462	6.142	5.847	5.575	5.324	5.092	4.876	4.675
16	7.379	6.974	6.604	6.265	5.954	5.668	5.405	5.162	4.938	4.730
17	7.549	7.120	6.729	6.373	6.047	5.749	5.475	5.222	4.990	4.775
18	7.702	7.250	6.840	6.467	6.128	5.818	5.534	5.273	5.033	4.812
19	7.839	7.366	6.938	6.550	6.198	5.877	5.584	5.316	5.070	4.843
20	7.963	7.469	7.025	6.623	6.259	5.929	5.628	5.353	5.101	4.870

Area under the normal curve

This table gives the area under the normal curve between the mean and the point Z standard deviations above the mean. The corresponding area for deviations below the mean can be found by symmetry.

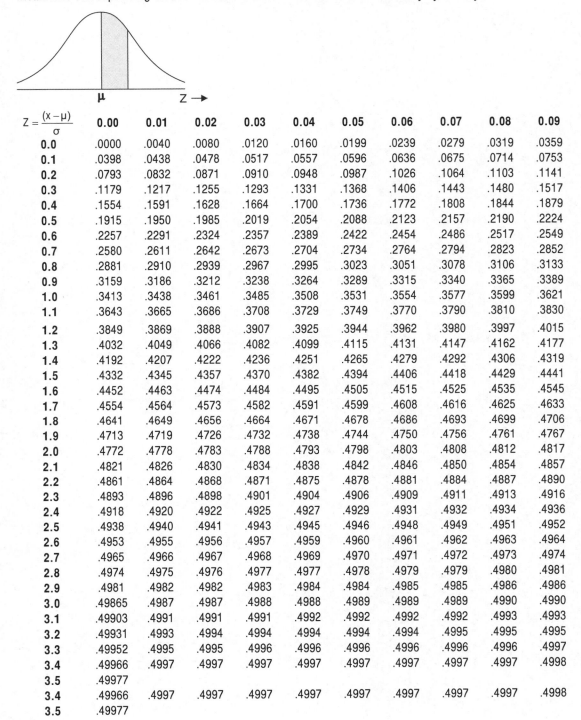

$$Z = \frac{(x - \mu)}{\sigma}$$

Z	0.00	0.01	0.02	0.03	0.04	0.05	0.06	0.07	0.08	0.09
0.0	.0000	.0040	.0080	.0120	.0160	.0199	.0239	.0279	.0319	.0359
0.1	.0398	.0438	.0478	.0517	.0557	.0596	.0636	.0675	.0714	.0753
0.2	.0793	.0832	.0871	.0910	.0948	.0987	.1026	.1064	.1103	.1141
0.3	.1179	.1217	.1255	.1293	.1331	.1368	.1406	.1443	.1480	.1517
0.4	.1554	.1591	.1628	.1664	.1700	.1736	.1772	.1808	.1844	.1879
0.5	.1915	.1950	.1985	.2019	.2054	.2088	.2123	.2157	.2190	.2224
0.6	.2257	.2291	.2324	.2357	.2389	.2422	.2454	.2486	.2517	.2549
0.7	.2580	.2611	.2642	.2673	.2704	.2734	.2764	.2794	.2823	.2852
0.8	.2881	.2910	.2939	.2967	.2995	.3023	.3051	.3078	.3106	.3133
0.9	.3159	.3186	.3212	.3238	.3264	.3289	.3315	.3340	.3365	.3389
1.0	.3413	.3438	.3461	.3485	.3508	.3531	.3554	.3577	.3599	.3621
1.1	.3643	.3665	.3686	.3708	.3729	.3749	.3770	.3790	.3810	.3830
1.2	.3849	.3869	.3888	.3907	.3925	.3944	.3962	.3980	.3997	.4015
1.3	.4032	.4049	.4066	.4082	.4099	.4115	.4131	.4147	.4162	.4177
1.4	.4192	.4207	.4222	.4236	.4251	.4265	.4279	.4292	.4306	.4319
1.5	.4332	.4345	.4357	.4370	.4382	.4394	.4406	.4418	.4429	.4441
1.6	.4452	.4463	.4474	.4484	.4495	.4505	.4515	.4525	.4535	.4545
1.7	.4554	.4564	.4573	.4582	.4591	.4599	.4608	.4616	.4625	.4633
1.8	.4641	.4649	.4656	.4664	.4671	.4678	.4686	.4693	.4699	.4706
1.9	.4713	.4719	.4726	.4732	.4738	.4744	.4750	.4756	.4761	.4767
2.0	.4772	.4778	.4783	.4788	.4793	.4798	.4803	.4808	.4812	.4817
2.1	.4821	.4826	.4830	.4834	.4838	.4842	.4846	.4850	.4854	.4857
2.2	.4861	.4864	.4868	.4871	.4875	.4878	.4881	.4884	.4887	.4890
2.3	.4893	.4896	.4898	.4901	.4904	.4906	.4909	.4911	.4913	.4916
2.4	.4918	.4920	.4922	.4925	.4927	.4929	.4931	.4932	.4934	.4936
2.5	.4938	.4940	.4941	.4943	.4945	.4946	.4948	.4949	.4951	.4952
2.6	.4953	.4955	.4956	.4957	.4959	.4960	.4961	.4962	.4963	.4964
2.7	.4965	.4966	.4967	.4968	.4969	.4970	.4971	.4972	.4973	.4974
2.8	.4974	.4975	.4976	.4977	.4977	.4978	.4979	.4979	.4980	.4981
2.9	.4981	.4982	.4982	.4983	.4984	.4984	.4985	.4985	.4986	.4986
3.0	.49865	.4987	.4987	.4988	.4988	.4989	.4989	.4989	.4990	.4990
3.1	.49903	.4991	.4991	.4991	.4992	.4992	.4992	.4992	.4993	.4993
3.2	.49931	.4993	.4994	.4994	.4994	.4994	.4994	.4995	.4995	.4995
3.3	.49952	.4995	.4995	.4996	.4996	.4996	.4996	.4996	.4996	.4997
3.4	.49966	.4997	.4997	.4997	.4997	.4997	.4997	.4997	.4997	.4998
3.5	.49977									
3.4	.49966	.4997	.4997	.4997	.4997	.4997	.4997	.4997	.4997	.4998
3.5	.49977									

Suggested formulae to learn

Chapter 1: Absorption costing and activity based costing

$$OAR = \frac{\text{Estimated overhead costs}}{\text{Expected (normal) activity level}}$$

Actual overhead expenditure	X
Amount of overhead absorbed (OAR × actual activity level)	(X)
Under/(over) absorption	X/(X)

Chapter 2: Marginal costing and throughput accounting

Contribution per unit = selling price per unit less all variable costs per unit

or

Total contribution = total sales revenue less total variable costs

Difference between absorption costing profit and marginal costing profit = OAR/unit × movement in inventory

Throughput contribution = sales revenue − direct material cost

Chapter 5: Multi-product breakeven analysis

Single product:

$$\text{Breakeven point (units)} = \frac{\text{Fixed costs}}{\text{Unit contribution}}$$

$$\text{Contribution/Sales ratio (C/S ratio)} = \frac{\text{Contribution / unit}}{\text{Selling price / unit}}$$

$$\text{Breakeven revenue} = \frac{\text{Fixed costs}}{\text{C / S ratio}} \quad \text{or} \quad \text{Breakeven point} \times \text{selling price/unit}$$

$$\text{Output required for target profit} = \frac{\text{Fixed costs + target profit}}{\text{Unit contribution}}$$

Margin of safety = Budgeted sales − Breakeven sales

$$\text{Margin of safety (\%)} = \frac{\text{Budgeted sales} - \text{Breakeven sales}}{\text{Budgeted sales}}$$

Multi-product:

$$\text{Breakeven point} = \frac{\text{Fixed costs}}{\text{Weighted average unit contribution}}$$

$$\text{Breakeven revenue} = \frac{\text{Fixed costs}}{\text{Weighted average C/S ratio}}$$

Chapter 8: Risk and uncertainty in decision-making

$EV = \Sigma px$

Where p is the probability of the outcome occurring, and x is the value of that outcome

Standard deviation = $\quad \sigma = \sqrt{\Sigma p(x - \overline{x})^2} = \sqrt{\Sigma p(x - EV)^2}$

Coefficient of variation = $\dfrac{\sigma}{EV}$

Value of perfect information (VOPI)

EV (with perfect information)	X
EV (no perfect information)	(X)
VOPI	X

Chapter 9: Forecasting techniques

Time series models:

Additive model: TS = T + SV
Multiplicative model: TS = T x SV

Linear regression:

To calculate the values of a and b for the straight line expression y = a + bx, the following formulae are used:

$b = \dfrac{n\Sigma xy - \Sigma x \Sigma y}{n\Sigma x^2 - (\Sigma x)^2}$

$a = \quad \overline{y} - b\,\overline{x} \quad (\text{or } a = \dfrac{y}{n} - b\dfrac{x}{n})$

where n is the number of pairs of observations.

Correlation coefficient: $r = \dfrac{n\Sigma xy - \Sigma x \Sigma y}{\sqrt{[n\Sigma x^2 - (\Sigma x)^2][n\Sigma y^2 - (\Sigma y)^2]}}$

The coefficient of determination = r^2

Note that it is unlikely that you would be expected to remember the linear regression formulae in the exam and the formulae would probably be provided within the question.

Chapter 10: Budgeting for planning

Inventory adjustments:

Finished Goods (FG)   *Raw Materials (RM)*

	Units		Kg/litres
Sales	X	Usage	X
+ Closing inventory (FG)	X	+ Closing inventory (RM)	X
– Opening inventory (FG)	(X)	– Opening inventory (RM)	(X)
Production	X	Purchases	X

BPP LEARNING MEDIA

Chapter 12: Standard costing and variance analysis

Material variances

			$
Price	–	Based on actual purchases	
		What should they have cost?	X
		What did they cost?	(X)
			X

			Kg
Usage	–	Based on actual production	
		What should it have used?	X
		What did it use?	(X)
			X
		Difference valued at standard cost per kg	$X

Labour variances

			$
Rate	–	Based on actual hours paid	
		What should they have cost?	X
		What did they cost?	(X)
			X

			Hrs
Efficiency	–	Based on actual production units	
		How long should it have taken?	X
		How long did it take?	(X)
			X
		Difference valued at standard rate per hour	$X

			Hrs
Idle time	–	Hours worked	X
		Hours paid	(X)
		Difference valued at standard rate per hour	$X

Variable overhead variances

			$
Expenditure	–	Based on actual hours worked	
		What should they have cost?	X
		What did they cost?	(X)
			X

			Hrs
Efficiency	–	Based on actual production units	
		How long should it have taken?	X
		How long did it take?	(X)
			X
		Difference valued at standard rate per hour	$X

Note. This assumes variable overheads are incurred per labour hour.

Fixed overhead variances

Total variance
(Over/under absorption)

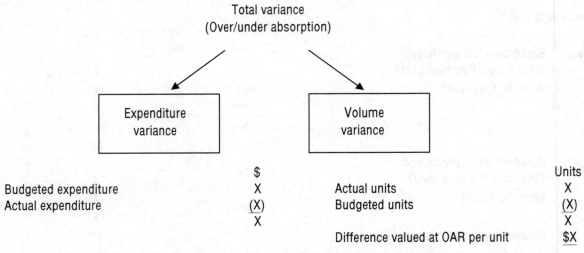

	$		Units
Budgeted expenditure	X	Actual units	X
Actual expenditure	(X)	Budgeted units	(X)
	X		X
		Difference valued at OAR per unit	$X

The fixed overhead volume variance can be subdivided into the capacity and the efficiency variance.

Capacity variance:

	Hours
Budgeted hours for budgeted units	X
Actual hours	(X)
	X
Difference valued at OAR per hour	$X

Efficiency variance

	Hours
	X
Standard hours for actual production units	(X)
Actual hours	X
	$X

Difference valued at OAR per hour

Sales variances

Price –	Based on actual units sold	$
	What should they sell for?	X
	What did they sell for?	(X)
		X

Volume –	Based on actual units sold	Units
	Budgeted sales	X
	Actual sales	(X)
		X
	Difference valued at standard contribution/unit	$X

Under absorption costing this variance will be valued at standard **profit**/unit.

Chapter 12: Further variance analysis

Mix variance

	Actual quantity at standard mix	Actual quantity at actual mix	Difference (kg)	Standard cost ($)	Variance ($)
Ingredient 1					
Ingredient 2					
Total					

Yield variance

	Standard quantity at standard mix	Actual quantity at standard mix	Difference (kg)	Standard cost ($)	Variance ($)
Ingredient 1					
Ingredient 2					
Total					

Operational variances

(i)

Actual production should take (× number of hours)	X hours
but did take	X hours
Efficiency variance in hours	X hours (A/F)
× revised standard cost per hour	× $X (A/F)
Efficiency variance in $	X (A/F)

(ii)

	$
Revised standard price of actual hours paid	X
Actual price of actual hours paid	X
Rate variance	X (A/F)

(iii)   **Check**

	$
Revised standard cost for revised std hrs	X
Actual costs	X
Total operational variance (i) + (ii)	X (A/F)

Planning variance

	$
Revised standard cost for revised standard hours for actual o/put	X
Original standard cost for original standard hours for actual o/put	X
Total planning variance	X (A/F)

Planning rate variance

	$
Original standard cost for revised standard hours for actual output	X
Revised standard cost for revised standard hours for actual output	X
Planning rate variance	X (A/F)

Planning efficiency variance

The original standard hours for actual output were	X
The revised standard hours for actual output are	X
Labour efficiency planning variance in hours	(A/F)
× original standard rate per hour	× $X
Labour efficiency planning variance in $	X (A/F)

BPP
LEARNING MEDIA